THE WRITINGS OF ST. PATRICK

The Apostle of Ireland.

THE WRITINGS
OF ST. PATRICK

The Apostle of Ireland

A REVISED TRANSLATION WITH NOTES
CRITICAL AND HISTORICAL

BY THE

Rev. CHARLES H. H. WRIGHT, D.D.

*Trin. Coll., Dublin, M.A. of Exeter Coll., Oxford,
Ph.D. of University of Leipzig, Donnellan Lecturer (1880–81) in University of Dublin, Exa-
miner in the University of London,
Bampton Lecturer (1878), and Grin-
field Lecturer on the LXX. in the
University of Oxford.*

Fredonia Books
Amsterdam, The Netherlands

The Writings of St. Patrick:
The Apostle of Ireland

by
Charles H. H. Wright

ISBN: 1-4101-0338-2

Fredonia Books
Amsterdam, The Netherlands
http://www.fredoniabooks.com

Contents.

		PAGE
I. INTRODUCTION	. . . .	7
II. BRIEF SKETCH OF ST. PATRICK'S LIFE	. .	30
III. GENUINE WRITINGS OF PATRICK.		
(a) The Hymn, or 'Breastplate'	. . .	42
(b) The Confession	. . . .	46
(c) Epistle to Coroticus	. . . .	73
IV. DOUBTFUL REMAINS.		
(a) Sayings of Patrick	. . . .	81
(b) Proverbs of Patrick	. . . .	86
(c) The Story of Patrick and the Royal Daughters		90
(d) Patrick's Vision of the Future of Ireland	.	95
(e) A Confession attributed to St. Patrick, from the		
Revue Celtique	. . . . .	99

Contents.

PAGE

V. APPENDIX—POETICAL VERSIONS OF THE HYMN.

    (*a*) Version of James Clarence Mangan .   . 110

    (*b*) Version of Mrs. Alexander   .   .   114

    (*c*) Version of Joseph John Murphy .   . 117

Notes on Patrick's Hymn 120

   ,,   ,,   Confession 123

   ,,   ,,   Epistle to Coroticus .   .   . 143

   ,,   The Confession of Tours .   .   . 148

VI. THE ANCIENT IRISH HYMN IN THE ORIGINAL IRISH,
     WITH A TRANSLATION INTO MODERN IRISH, BY
     THE LATE REV. PROFESSOR GOODMAN, M.A. .   . 150

Introduction.

THE present edition of the writings of St. Patrick is an attempt to bring out in English the works of that great man, with the necessary addition of historical and critical notes, but with the omission, as far as possible, of all matter which has been made the subject of religious controversy. In the earlier editions of this work, which were issued nominally under the joint editorship of Rev. G. T. Stokes, D.D., Professor of Ecclesiastical History in the University of Dublin, and myself, a special attempt was indeed made to avoid touching upon every point likely to arouse controversy. It was hoped that an impartial edition of Patrick's works without controversial notes or comments might have been useful and acceptable to Irishmen of

various creeds and opinions, as well as to English
Christians, who, in general, know little of the
great Apostle of Ireland.*

The utter impossibility of publishing in Ireland
any work of the kind which would be regarded
with equal favour by Roman Catholics and Protestants was abundantly proved in this case.   An
eminent Irish scholar, a Roman Catholic priest,
who died some time after the publication of the
earlier editions, was asked to join with me as
co-editor of the work, in order to secure its
impartiality.   He, however, stated that he could
not approve of publishing St. Patrick's writings
without theological notes, and that he would
require to be permitted to point out that even
the occasional use by Patrick of the term *sacerdos*
(priest) to indicate a Christian minister was sufficient to prove that St. Patrick believed in the
Roman Catholic doctrine of ' the sacrifice of the
mass.'   Of course under such conditions it was
impossible to accept his services.   The *Irish
Catholic*, a Dublin Roman Catholic weekly
journal, in a review of the work after its publication, similarly maintained that the omission in
the work of any discussion of the   question

* These expectations were not wholly unfulfilled.   Four thousand copies of an 8vo. edition in pica type, published at sixpence
sewn, and one shilling in cloth, were disposed of in a little more
than eighteen months.   This in itself must be regarded as a very
creditable fact.   But the price at which the work had been issued
was unremunerative, and although a sum of £30 was subscribed
in answer to an appeal by the Irish Branch of the Evangelical
Alliance, that sum was wholly insufficient to print successive
editions of the work, and to meet other necessary expenses.   Hence
the work was offered to the Religious Tract Society, and accepted
by that Society for publication in their 'Christian Classics' Series.

whether Patrick received a commission from Rome or not was simply 'the suppression of everything in the shape of argument on the Catholic side!' The work, however, was, on publication, warmly commended by a Roman Catholic prelate in Ireland, but he declined to permit his commendation to be published.

There is no allusion whatever in St. Patrick's writings to his having received any commission from the Pope. If, therefore, he did receive a commission from Rome—a point on which no trustworthy evidence can be adduced—the silence of Patrick on the subject would prove that he attached no such importance to such a commission as his mediæval biographers were disposed to affirm. But, as Dr. Stokes has well pointed out, in his work on *Ireland and the Celtic Church* (p. 51), the question is, from a Protestant standpoint, of little importance, and if the evidence brought forward in favour of the Roman claim were strong enough we should have no hesitation whatever in admitting the point.

Those who are interested in such investigations can easily consult for themselves the arguments brought forward on the subject in Professor G. T. Stokes' work, and dwelt upon with more fulness of detail in Dr. Todd's *St. Patrick, the Apostle of Ireland*. It is, therefore, unnecessary here to enter upon that thorny subject of discussion. It may be, however, noted in passing, that the first of 'the sayings of Patrick' preserved in the Book of Armagh, and given in the present volume among the doubtful remains of the saint, alludes to the fact of Patrick's having visited Italy.

There is nothing, however, to show where those *Dicta* came from, and therefore they cannot be regarded as conclusive evidence. It is, however, quite true that St. Patrick's autobiography, as set forth in his *Confession*, passes over in silence the events of many years.

In the present work the Latin term *sacerdos* has been invariably translated 'priest,' *presbyterus* has been rendered 'presbyter,' and *clerici* 'clergy.' In some of the Roman Catholic editions the latter term has been translated 'priests.'

It must be observed that early Celtic Christianity was very different in its external form from the Christianity of modern times, whether Roman Catholic or Protestant. Many usages which were afterwards distinct features of the Celtic Church of Ireland, and which appear to have been the growth of later days, are not alluded to in Patrick's writings. St. Patrick's writings are indeed brief and scanty, but are clear enough on the essential points of Christian doctrine. No such exaggerated views on the celibacy of the clergy were held by Patrick as were afterwards prevalent, for he mentions without scruple the fact that both his father and grandfather were clergymen. On the other hand, he speaks with approval of monks and virgins, which were not in his days recluses like those described in Professor G. T. Stokes' ninth lecture. Patrick also quotes passages of the Old Testament apocryphal books which he evidently viewed as inspired Scripture. In spite of all these drawbacks, as Protestants must regard them, the writings of the saint are in the main strongly evangelical, and cannot fail to be perused by all Christians with both pleasure and profit.

In the present edition we have divided the 'remains' of Patrick into two divisions; the first containing the writings which are probably genuine, the second a few remains of interest which are of doubtful genuineness, but which are, notwithstanding, of considerable interest, and not generally known.

The genuine writings are three in number, namely, Patrick's *Hymn*, his *Confession*, and his *Epistle to Coroticus*. The doubtful remains are (1) the *Dicta Patricii*, contained in folio 9, a 1, of the Book of Armagh. Their rustic Latinity is some evidence in their favour, though not absolutely conclusive. (2) *The Proverbs of Patrick* are also of doubtful authorship. There are some strong points in their favour, but it is impossible now to test the statement of the monk Jocelin that they were translated from Irish into Latin. (3) The interview of Patrick with the daughters of King Loegaire, if not certainly a Patrician document, possesses marks of high antiquity. (4) *Patrick's Vision of Ireland's Future* stands in such marked contrast with the fables in which it is imbedded that it is worth preserving, though not likely to have been authentic. (5) We have added to this edition the remarkable *Confession* found at Angers, but probably belonging originally to Tours, to which we have appended introductory remarks.

There are other works ascribed to Patrick which, however, have been shown to be spurious

by competent scholars. These are to be found
in Patrick's *Opuscula*, edited by Ware * and
Villanueva.† No scholar, however, who has
read even a few lines of the tract *De Tribus
Habitaculis, Of the Three Habitations* (or the
World, Heaven, and Hell), could believe St.
Patrick to have been its author, so different
in all respects is its Latin style from that
exhibited in the genuine *Confessio* and *Coroticus*.
The same may be said of the tract *De abusionibus
Seculi*, and of others. Some, if not all, of the
Canons attributed to Patrick are decidedly pro-
ductions of a later age. None of them, in the
form in which they have come down to us, are
earlier than the eighth century. See Dr. Todd's
St. Patrick, pp. 485 ff., and Dr. W. Stokes in
the *Tripartite Life*, as also the article by Professor
G. T. Stokes, in Smith and Wace's *Dict. of
Christian Biography*.

St. Patrick's Irish *Hymn* is of great antiquity,
although, as Dr. Todd says, ' it may be difficult,
if not impossible, to adduce *proof* in support
of the tradition that Patrick was its author.'
The Irish hymn is distinctly mentioned in
Tirechán's *Collections*, that is, in the middle of
the seventh century.‡ It is a composition of

* *St. Patricii qui Hibernos ad fidem Christi convertit adscripta
Opuscula.* Opera et studio J. Waræi, Eq. Aur. Lond. 1656.
† *Sancti Patricii, Ibernorum Apostoli. Synodi, Canones, Opuscula
et Scriptorum qui supersunt Fragmenta:* scholiis illustr. a Joachimo
Laurentio Villanueva, Presbyt. Dublini apud R. Graisberry,
1835.
‡ Tirechán is said to have written his *Collections* of matters
connected with St. Patrick 'from the lips or book' of Ultan
(died 656), whose pupil he was. This Ultan was (A.D. 652)

considerable force and beauty, written at a time
when Paganism was almost supreme in Ireland.
The author shared in the general belief of the
day that even heathen sorcerers had mysterious
powers by which they could work harm to their
opponents. The expressions used in the *Hymn*
correspond with the circumstances under which
Patrick set out on his missionary visit to Tara to
confront in its own stronghold the idolatry which
was then rampant in the land.* The very expression 'Creator of doom' in reference to God
which occurs twice in the *Hymn* is evidence
in favour of its Patrician authorship. For,
according to the *Tripartite Life*, which embodies
some fragments of antiquity, 'my God's doom,'

Bishop of Clonard, which in later times formed part of the diocese
of Meath. The *Collections* of Tirechán form part of the miscel-
laneous matter contained in the MS. known as the Book of
Armagh. According to Tirechán, four special honours were to be
paid to him in all the monasteries and churches of Ireland.
1. The festival of St. Patrick's death, though in Lent (March 17),
was to be celebrated by three days' festivities, during which all
kinds of good food and flesh meat might lawfully be partaken of.
2. There a special mass was to be offered up in his honour on
that day (*offertorium ejus proprium in eodem die immolari*). 3. The
hymn of Secundinus, written in honour of St. Patrick, was to be
sung during the whole time. 4. At all times of the year they
were to sing Patrick's Irish hymn (*canticum ejus scotticum semper
canere*). See Dr. Whitley Stokes, *Tripartite Life of St. Patrick*,
p. 333.

* It was on this occasion that St. Patrick is related, in the later
legend, to have illustrated the doctrine of the Trinity by the three
leaves united into one in the shamrock. Dr. Fowler, in his
edition of *Adamnan's Life of S. Columba* (p. xxxiii.), observes
on the latter point : 'The use of the trefoil as an emblem in
Ireland is very ancient, but probably of pagan origin. None of
the early or mediæval Lives, however, connect it with St. Patrick,
and the legend seems not to be found earlier than A.D. 1600. It
is not mentioned by Colgan, who wrote in 1647.'

or 'the doom' and 'judgment of my God,' appears to have been one of Patrick's favourite expressions, to which he constantly gave utterance. It is noteworthy, too, that whereas, according to the later legends, Patrick was conscious of possessing extraordinary powers of performing miracles—miracles greater than those performed by the Apostles of Christ—Patrick, in his *Hymn*, in full anticipation of the dangers which surrounded him, relied on no such powers, but speaks of the protecting hand of that God who has ever been a refuge and strength to His people (Psa. xlvi.). It cannot be denied that even the two earliest memoirs of the saint contained in the Book of Armagh, which MS. was written itself in A.D. 807 (see p. 20), namely, the memoir by Muirchu Maccu-Machthéni, and that by Tirechán, written scarcely later than two centuries after Patrick's death, speak of marvellous displays of miraculous power (see p. 16). No such references to miraculous agency can, however, be detected in the poem, and it is therefore probable that it is of a considerably earlier date than those memoirs.

The *Hymn* in the original is written in a very ancient dialect of Irish, and hence the meaning of some words and phrases is somewhat uncertain. It is one of those compositions termed by the Latin name of *Lorica*, or 'breastplate,' the repetition of which was supposed to guard a traveller like a breastplate from spiritual foes. This popular belief is alluded to in the Irish preface, which will be found in note 1 on the *Hymn*. The translation of the *Hymn* in our

first edition was taken from that set forth by
Dr. Todd in his *St. Patrick*, pp. 426-9.* The
translation there given was mainly the work of
Whitley Stokes, and was a great advance upon
the earliest version given by Dr. Petrie (see
notes on *Hymn* at the end of book). The translation in the present work is in the main the
improved version of Dr. Whitley Stokes. The
alterations made in the older translation are all
noted, and the grounds for them set forth in the
critical notes. There are two MSS. of the
Hymn, one in the *Liber Hymnorum* in the
Library of Trinity College, Dublin, the other
in the Bodleian copy of the *Tripartite Life*.
The *Hymn* of Patrick has been set to music as
a sacred cantata by the late Sir Robert Stewart,
Professor of Music in the University of Dublin,
and was performed for the first time in St.
Patrick's Cathedral, Dublin, on St. Patrick's Day,
March 17, 1888. See remarks on Mrs. Alex-
ander's Version, p. 110.

In the present edition we have given the
hymn in the ancient Irish from the MS. in
Trinity College, Dublin, accompanied by a translation of it into the modern Irish language. The
latter translation has been made by the late Rev.
James Goodman, M.A., Professor of Irish in the

---

* *St. Patrick, Apostle of Ireland: A Memoir of his Life and
Mission*, with an Introductory Dissertation on some early usages
of the Church in Ireland, and its historical position from the
establishment of the English Colony to the present day. By
James Henthorn Todd, D.D., Senior Fellow of Trinity College,
Regius Prof. of Hebrew in the University, and Treasurer of St.
Patrick's Cathedral, Dublin. Dublin: Hodges, Smith & Co.
1864.

University of Dublin, one of whose last acts was
to revise the proof-sheet of that translation.

The other works of Patrick acknowledged
to be genuine are the *Confession* and the *Epistle
to Coroticus*. The evidence in favour of the
authenticity of those documents is, as curtly
stated by Dr. Whitley Stokes, five-fold. Rolls
Tripartite, p. xciii. (1) The mention of decurions. See *Coroticus*, § 5, and note, p. 145.
(2) The use of the plural word Brittanniæ, or
Britains. See *Confession*, § 10, and note 6,
p. 134. (3) The Biblical quotations are made in
both documents from an ante-Hieronymian
version of the Bible. (4) The *Confession* speaks
of a married clergy ; and (5) the Latin style
used in both documents is very similar to that
found in the writings of Gregory of Tours, who
was a missionary from Ireland. See p. 24. In
addition to these five points, it may be added
that (6) the references to the events of the age
correspond with facts known from other sources.
(See Professor G. T. Stokes' notes on the *Confession*, chap. i. pp. 125, 126; chap. ii. p. 131 ; and
on *Coroticus*, pp. 143, 144 ; &c.) Moreover (7),
the utter absence of any references to miracles
in both writings (although miracles abound, as
already noticed, in all the later biographies) is
additional proof that those documents are genuine
remains of the Apostle of Ireland.

The utter absence of ' the marvellous ' in the
Confession and *Epistle to Coroticus* is the more
remarkable when it is borne in mind that the
notes on Patrick's life by Muirchu Maccu-
Machthéni, which is found in the Book or

Armagh, speak of the miracles performed by him at Tara, when contending with the magicians of King Loegaire. Those notes relate the miracle of Patrick's raising Daire's horse to life after it had died on account of trespassing on the ground given by Daire to Patrick at Armagh for religious purposes. They tell of a dead man speaking to Patrick out of his grave ; of an angel who appeared to Patrick, as to Moses, in a burning bush ; and other like wonders. The date of Muirchu is about A.D. 690. The collections of Tirechán, who probably lived about the same date, and are also contained in the Book of Armagh, relate also many miracles. Tirechán distinctly quotes from the *Confession*.

The *Tripartite Life*, probably composed in the eleventh century, contains even more marvels ; as does also the later life drawn up by Jocelin, a monk of the twelfth century. According to Jocelin, Patrick was baptized by a blind priest, who obtained the water required for the purpose by causing the infant to make the sign of the cross over the earth, when a well of water gushed forth, which not only cured the priest of his blindness, but enabled him to read the order of baptism 'without knowing until then his letters.' Icicles are said to have been transformed by Patrick into faggots, butter changed into honey. The saint was able, like Christ after His resurrection, to pass through shut doors. When his horses were lost on one occasion, 'St. Patrick raised up his hand ; his five fingers illumined the whole plain as if they were five lamps, and the horses were found at

2

once.' A goat bleated in the stomachs of
the men who had eaten it up, and, according
to a still later embellishment, came forth alive
out of their mouths. When a tooth fell out of
Patrick's head as he was crossing a river, the
tooth shone in the ford like a sun ; and on
another occasion Coroticus, the king of the
Britons, was changed by him into a fox. The
man Victoricus, whom St. Patrick relates he saw
in a dream (p. 57), is transformed in the later
legends into his guardian angel Victor !

In opposition to all such marvels, the autobiography contained in the *Confession*, and the
statements made in the *Epistle to Coroticus*, are
distinguished by a sobriety of narration which
in itself goes far to prove their genuineness.
Not even the legend-loving scribes of a later age
have dared to interpolate those writings with
their absurd wonders.

Among the various works which contain
translations of these writings of Patrick, Miss
Cusack's *Life of St. Patrick* * is of special interest,
as the ablest and largest work on the subject
written from a Roman Catholic standpoint.
Miss Cusack has left the Church of Rome
since these lines were originally penned. The
peculiar importance of her work in connection
with the Remains of Patrick consists in the fact
that it contains (pp. 369–502) the *Tripartite
Life of Saint Patrick, Apostle of Ireland,* translated
from the original Irish by W. M. Hennessy,
Esq., M.R.I.A. Mr. Hennessy gives the Latin

---

* *Life of St. Patrick, Apostle of Ireland.* By M. F. Cusack.
London : Longmans, Green & Co. 1871.

text of the *Confession* and *Epistle to Coroticus,* as
well as an English translation of both, with
some critical notes. Mr. Hennessy's death,
which occurred in January, 1889, has removed
from our midst one long known as a distinguished Irish scholar. He occupied the
position of Deputy-Keeper of the Records,
Ireland, and was favourably known by his
learned edition of the *Chronicon Scotorum,* in the
Rolls series.

An earlier translation into English of the
Confession of St. Patrick, written from a Roman
Catholic standpoint, is that by Archdeacon
Hamilton, printed and published by John C.
O'Reilly, 139, Capel Street, Dublin, in 1859.
Archdeacon Hamilton was at that time Roman
Catholic parish priest of St. Michan's, Dublin.
We have frequently referred to this translation
in the notes appended to the present work.

The most important work on the subject of
the Patrician writings is unquestionably the Rolls
edition of the *Tripartite Life,* and other documents relating to Patrick, by Dr Whitley
Stokes.* It contains among other matters a
translation of the *Hymn* with the original Irish,
and the Latin text of the *Confession,* from the
Book of Armagh and the Cottonian MS., with
the *Dicta Patricii.* The *Epistle to Coroticus,*

---

* *The Tripartite Life of St. Patrick, with other Documents relating to that Saint.* Edited with Translations and Indexes by
Whitley Stokes, D.C.L., LL.D., Hon. Fellow of Jesus College,
Oxford. Parts I. and II. London. Published under the
direction of the Master of the Rolls, by Eyre and Spottiswoode.
1887.

which is not contained in the Book of Armagh,
is given here from the Cottonian MS.

The Latin text of the *Confession*, as found in
the Book of Armagh, and in the Bodleian MS.
Fell. 1, has also been published in Gilbert's
(John, F.S.A., M.R.I.A.) splendid work, *Facsimiles of the National MSS. of Ireland*, Part II.
London. 1878. Published under the direction
of the Master of the Rolls. Another critical
edition of the Latin *Confession* with various
readings is contained in Haddan and Stubbs'
Councils and Ecclesiastical Documents, vol. ii.
part ii. These works have not, however, generally speaking, been consulted in the preparation
of the present volume, as Dr. Whitley Stokes'
work rendered that examination unnecessary.

The Book of Armagh has been proved by
Bishop Graves, of Limerick, from internal evidence to have been written A.D. 807. The very
name of the scribe has been recovered.* That
codex is in itself a veritable miscellany. It contains, as already mentioned, two early memoirs
of Patrick, the *Dicta Patricii*, notes on various
subjects, the so-called *Liber Angeli*, relating to
the See of Armagh, the *Confessio* of Patrick,
Jerome's Preface to the Gospels, the Books of
the New Testament in full, with the apocryphal
Epistle to the Laodiceans ; and a life of Martin,
with dialogues and Epistles of the saint, &c.
The *Confessio* found in that codex was tran-
scribed from a MS. said to have been in
Patrick's own hand, and which certainly was

---

* See his paper in the Proceedings of the Royal Irish Academy,
III. pp. 316-324, and Whitley Stokes, Rolls *Tripartite*, p. xc.

difficult to read from age, for the copyist mentions
that fact several times.* It now forms part of
the treasures of the Library of Trinity College,
Dublin. The copy of this MS. used by Mr.
Hennessy was executed by Rev. Thaddeus
O'Mahony, D.D., Professor of Irish in the
University of Dublin from 1861 to 1879. The
text of the *Confession* in the Book of Armagh is
considerably shorter than that presented in other
MSS. Sir Samuel Ferguson is, however, most
probably correct in maintaining that 'that tran-
script [the Book of Armagh] bears many internal
evidences of an abridgment'; and there is nothing
in the more copious matter of the other copies
necessarily at variance with it, so far as it has
come down to us. Mr. Olden, whose work
will be found mentioned on p. 23, has given
substantial reasons to show that the copyist of
the Armagh MS., which was compiled with the
object of exalting the dignity of Armagh, in-
tentionally omitted passages in the *Confession*,
which the scribe supposed to be inconsistent with
the particular object he had in view. It is sad
to think that the earliest MS. labours under such
suspicion. The portions of the text added from
other MSS. have been supplied within square
brackets [ ] in the present work.

Four other MSS. of the *Confession* are known
to be in existence, namely, the Cottonian MS.
in the British Museum, and two Fell MSS. in
the Bodleian Library. These three MSS. are
assigned by Whitley Stokes to the eleventh

* See Dr. Todd's *St. Patrick*, p. 347.

century. The text, however, contained in the
folio volume of the *Acta Sanctorum*, published by
the Bollandist Fathers (Antwerp, 1668), was
taken from a MS. which was supposed by
Nicholson to have perished in the troublous
times of the French Revolution. That MS.
has, however, as the late Bishop of Down and
Connor (Dr. Reeves) informed me, been discovered near its old locality, the Monastery of
Vedastin or Saint Waast, near Arras, in the
North of France, and is now preserved in the
Public Library of Arras. (See also the Rolls
Tripartite, p. xciii.) The Latin texts given by
R. Steele Nicholson in his work on Patrick *
are those of the Cottonian MS. and the Bol-
landist text.

The text followed in the present edition is
substantially that given by Mr. Hennessy and
Dr. Whitley Stokes. It has been, however,
occasionally verified by reference to the Book
of Armagh, and has been constantly compared
with the other texts. The selection of various
readings given in the notes has been generally
taken from Mr. Hennessy's edition, or from
that of Dr. Whitley Stokes.

The following recent English translations of

---

* *St. Patrick: Apostle of Ireland in the Third Century*; The
story of his mission by Pope Celestine in A.D. 431, and of his
connection with the Church of Rome proved to be a mere fiction :
with an Appendix containing his Confession and Epistle to
Coroticus translated into English. By R. Steele Nicholson,
M.A., T.C.D. Dublin: McGlashan and Gill, 1868. Mr.
Nicholson's hypothesis that Patrick lived in the third century is
incidentally disproved by several of the historical points noticed
by Professor G. T. Stokes in his notes.

the Latin texts have been compared in drawing up the revised translation here given—(1) The translation of Mr. Hennessy contained in Miss Cusack's work ; (2) The translation of the *Confession* by Archdeacon Hamilton, noted on p. 17 ; (3) That of the Rev. Thomas Olden ; * (4) That by A. F. Foster,† and (5) last, but not least in importance, the translation into English blank verse by the lately deceased, and much-to-be-regretted, Sir Samuel Ferguson, LL.D., President of the Royal Irish Academy.‡

Owing to his long-continued separation from civilised life, and his constant use of the Irish language, the Latin of St. Patrick's writings is bad and ungrammatical. His style is also often broken, and occasionally obscure. This has created no little difficulty, and consequently all translators of his works have taken more or less liberties in their endeavours to present to their readers a readable English translation. A trans-

---

* *The Epistles and Hymn of St. Patrick, with the Contemporary Poem in his Praise by Secundinus,* translated into English. Edited by Rev. Thomas Olden, M.A., M.R.I.A., Vicar of Ballyclough. Third Edition, revised. London : Society for Promoting Christian Knowledge. 1894.

† *The Confession of St. Patrick; or, St. Patrick's Epistle to the Irish People in the Third Century.* Translated from copies of MSS. in the British Museum and the Bodleian Library at Oxford. With Introduction and Appendix by A. F. Foster. Glasgow : Printed at the University Press by Robert Maclehose, 153, West Nile Street. Mr. Foster has in many places not at all closely followed the original text.

‡ The Transactions of the Royal Irish Academy—Vol. xxvii. Polite Literature and Antiquities—VI. *On the Patrician Documents.* By Sir Samuel Ferguson, LL.D. Dublin : Published by the Academy. 1885. Since the death of Sir S. Ferguson, a later edition has been issued by Lady Ferguson.

lator who desires to be peculiarly faithful is
sometimes embarrassed in an attempt to translate such an author. In revising the English
translation for our edition, it has been sometimes
necessary to replace smooth English by English
of more questionable correctness and taste.
The ruggedness in some places of our revised
translation has been caused by the desire above
all things to be faithful. Had our author
expressed himself in grammatical Latin, we
should not have been satisfied with rugged
English. But the case is wholly altered when
one has to deal with works written in indif-
ferent Latin, and which it is desirable to translate as faithfully as possible. In his attempt
to be faithful, the late Mr. Hennessy frequently
left himself open to the same criticism.

The rude and ungrammatical character of
Patrick's Latin writings is a strong evidence of
their genuineness. New evidence, already
alluded to, has recently come to light indirectly
bearing on this point. A splendid edition of
the works of Gregory of Tours has lately been
published (1883–1885), edited by Arndt,
Bonnet, and Br. Krusch, in the *Monumenta
Germaniæ Historica*, giving for the first time
the nearest approach to the genuine text of
that Father. The Latin of Gregory is very
similar to that found in Patrick's writings.
Like the latter, it is semi-barbarous in grammar
and spelling. But it is exactly the Latin which
would be expected from a Celt educated in
Gaul.

Patrick's quotations from Holy Scripture also

cause some difficulty. It is probable that he often quoted from memory, and consequently not with verbal accuracy. And yet, after making all due allowance for this probability, we have considered it necessary to carefully examine his quotations from Scripture, and to compare them with the commonly received text of the Latin Vulgate and the older Latin version used by the early Latin Fathers, as edited by Sabatier, and designated generally as 'the Itala.' When the Latin text of Patrick's quotations agrees with the Vulgate, we have, as a matter of simple fair play, given the English text of the Douay Bible, so called because the Old Testament was published at Douay in 1600, the New Testament having been previously brought out at Rheims in 1582. As the Douay Bible is an accredited English translation of the Latin Vulgate, we have followed that Version, even in cases where we might as well (and possibly with better literary taste), have substituted the rendering of the Authorised Version as identical in meaning and more classical in style. But in cases where Patrick's quotations differ verbally from the Latin Vulgate the difference has been expressed in our translation. Patrick's Biblical quotations were made from a Latin Version earlier than that of Jerome. More might be said on this head if the ancient Irish Version of the New Testament in the Latin language, which forms the main portion of the Book of Armagh, had been published. Scholars are aware that a good commencement has been made in the way of

editing texts of portions of Latin translations
prior to that of Jerome. But the materials are
not yet at hand to enable anything satisfactory
to be done in the way of identifying the translation used by Patrick. Owing to the few
references made to the Gospels in Patrick's
Works, a comparison of his quotations of the
Gospels with Professor Abbott's *Evangeliorum
Versio Antehieronymiana* * yielded no result.

The division of the *Confession* into chapters
and sections has been in the main adopted from
the Bollandist edition. No such division is
found in the Book of Armagh. The contents
affixed to each chapter are, of course, our own.
Words supplied to complete the sense have been
as far as possible included in ordinary brackets
( ). The meaning of the square brackets [ ]
has been already explained on page 21.

Professor G. T. Stokes contributed to the
former edition certain notes of his own, which
reappear in the present edition with his name
attached to them. His numerous occupations
prevented him from taking more than a nominal
part in the editing of the former work, and
hence it was more satisfactory for me to
assume the responsibility of the sole editorship
of this edition.

* *Evangeliorum Versio Antehieronymiana* ex Codice Usseriano
(Dublinensi), adjecta collatione Codicis Usseriani Alterius.
Accedit Versio Vulgata sec. Cod. Amiatinum, cum varietate
Cod. Kenanensis (Book of Kells), et Cod. Durmachenis (Book
of Durrow). Edidit et praefatus est T. K. Abbott, S. T. B.,
Coll. SS. Trin. juxta Dublin, e Sociis ; Linguae Hebraicae et
Linguae Graecae Bibl. apud Dublinen Professor. 2 vols. Lond.,
1884.

Notwithstanding the ruggedness of style of Patrick's Latin works, and their want of accordance with grammatical rules, there is much to be commended in the simplicity and unadorned dignity of his narrative. The modesty and humility exhibited by him in the account given of the marvellous success of his mission is most remarkable. There is, moreover, in his writings a display of genuine missionary spirit, which, as it has roused many a Christian worker to action in the past, may well stir up many in our day also. Patrick everywhere displays an earnest trust and faith in the constant protection of a gracious Providence. His love for the souls of the men among whom he laboured, notwithstanding the ill-treatment he received at their hands, is remarkable. His honest simplicity and the contempt everywhere displayed for the riches of the world deserve far more general recognition than they have yet received. His acquaintance with the Holy Scripture, with the phraseology of which his Writings are thoroughly imbued, and his desire to conform his doctrine to their teaching, are significant.* To him God and

* It may be interesting as a proof of Patrick's love for the Scriptures to call attention to the remarkable reliquary known as the Domnach-airgid, or 'the silver shrine' which enclosed a copy of the Four Gospels in Latin, presented, according to the *Tripartite Life*, by Patrick to Aedh MacCarthenn of Clogher. The shrine and the manuscript it contained (which long belonged to the Monastery of Clones) are now among the most prized treasures of the Royal Irish Academy. The MS. is unfortunately for the most part a solid opaque mass ; portions of it, however, are still legible. It is highly probable that it was the veritable copy used by Patrick himself during his devotions. The 'shrine' is described by Dr. Petrie in vol. xviii. of the

Satan, heaven and hell, were great realities; ' he endured as seeing Him who is invisible' (Heb. xi. 27). Like Ignatius and many others, Patrick coveted earnestly to attain the crown of martyr-dom. His 'Creed' is clear and terse. A simple unaffected piety, wholly devoid of ostentation, breathes in every paragraph of his writings. He 'walked by faith,' and therefore his works were done in love. His writings ought to be dear to all lovers of the Gospel of Christ, to whatsoever creed they may severally belong. If we differ occasionally from his opinions, we learn at least to recognise that there is much precious truth held in common by those who do not think alike on all points of religion. There is a rugged eloquence in the *Epistle to Coroticus* which should come home to the hearts of all who read that stirring and manly rebuke ad-ministered by the Irish Apostle. It is, there-fore, earnestly to be hoped that the present edition of Patrick's Works may find its way into many Irish homes, and tend to endear the name of Patrick still more to all the people of Ireland. Not only Irishmen, but English and Scotchmen also, may read with pleasure and profit these short, but precious relics of a bygone age. Patrick's Works ought to be prized and valued by all those who delight in such devotional

Transactions of the Royal Irish Academy, where several plates are given of its sides. Facsimiles of the leaves which have been opened are given in Gilbert's *Facsimiles of the National MSS. of Ireland*, Part I. 1874, as well as in Eugene O'Curry's *Lectures on Manuscript Materials of Ancient Irish History*. Dublin: Duffy, 1861. The subject is referred to in Miss Cusack's *St. Patrick*, p. 431.

writings as *The Confessions* of Augustine or *The Imitation of Christ* of Thomas à Kempis. Much food will be found for the devotional life in the simple 'remains' of the Apostle of Ireland. May the study of the life and words of the humble disciple lead many to study still more deeply the life and teachings of the great Master Himself, whose words, recorded in the Gospels, 'are spirit and are life!' (John vi. 63.)

Brief Sketch of the Life of St. Patrick.

ST. PATRICK was probably born at Dumbarton (see p. 125) about A.D. 373 (Rolls *Tripartite*, p. cxxxvii.). His missionary work in Ireland does not seem to have begun until some time after A.D. 432 or 439. Prosper of Aquitaine, an intimate friend of Pope Celestine, flourished in the first half of the fifth century, and wrote a chronicle which extends to A.D. 455. In the older editions of that work the chronicle extended only to 433, but continuations of it have been discovered later. Prosper does not speak of the mission of St. Patrick the Apostle of Ireland, but mentions the mission of Palladius to Ireland in A.D. 431. This is recorded in the following terms : 'Palladius, ordained by Pope Celestine, is sent to the Scots believing in Christ (*ad Scotos in Christum credentes*) as first bishop.' These Scots were Irish (see Prof. G. T.

Stokes, note 23, p. 139). The mission of Palladius
proved unsuccessful, and Palladius himself died
shortly after. As Palladius was well known to
ancient Irish writers as the senior Patrick, it is
possible that his mission was in later times confused
with the more successful work of the so-called
Apostle of Ireland. Prosper was probably dead
ere the work of the latter evangelist was accomplished.

The language used by Prosper shows plainly
that both he and Pope Celestine were of opinion
that Christians in Ireland existed at that early
period. In later times, however, attempts were
made to conceal that fact. Hence, when the Irish
historian Nennius in 858 issued his edition of the
Historia Britonum, compiled probably in 822 (see
Rolls *Tripartite*, p. cxvii., and extracts, p. 498),
that writer corrects Prosper's language into 'the
Scots to be converted to Christ' (*ad Scottos in
Christum convertendos*), and in afterwards speaking
of St. Patrick's mission, which Nennius relates
as undertaken at the suggestion also of Pope Celestine, a similar expression is made use of, namely,
ad Scottos in fidem Christi convertendos mittitur, 'he
is sent to the Scots to be converted into the faith
of Christ.'

St. Patrick, as his name indicates, most probably
sprang from a Roman family which had settled in
'the Britains' (see note 2, p. 123, and note 6, p. 134).
According to the *Tripartite Life* his mother's name
was Concessa, a sister or relation of St. Martin of
Tours (Rolls *Trip.*, p. 8). The same statement
is made by the earlier writer Muirchu (Rolls
Trip., p. 494), and probably by St. Patrick himself
(see note 3, p. 124). She appears also to have been
of Roman origin. His father, grandfather, and

great-grandfather appear all to have been clergy-men (see note 4, p. 124), clerical celibacy not being enforced in those days. Patrick was carried off captive from his native land when sixteen years old, during one of the piratical descents of the Irish on the coasts of the Britains (see note 8, p. 126). He was then a stranger to true religion (see p. 47), which fact is elsewhere several times referred to (see note 9, p. 126). Muirchu, one of his earliest biographers, gives the same account. The later legends, which speak of Patrick's early piety and of miracles performed by him in his infancy and childhood, had not then come into existence.

The autobiography set forth in his *Confession* (chaps. i. and ii.) gives all that is really known about his early life, and concerning his captivity in Ireland, during which dark season of affliction he was brought to know the Lord (p. 47). There is, however, no mention made in the *Confession* of the place in which he was trained for the ministry, or of his ordination. That he was ' a deacon' at one time of his life, and was made a bishop at another, is there mentioned (pp. 58, 73). Patrick confesses, however, his lack of learning and of training for the ministry ; and though he was by nature a man of considerable intellectual gifts, his writings confirm his own statements with respect to the want of early education (see pp. 49, 67).

There are, however, considerable gaps in this autobiography. When we consider the pride he took in his noble birth, the high estimation in which he held the Roman and Gallic Christians (p. 77), the reference (in the doubtful ' sayings ') to the Roman style of chanting (pp. 83, 84), it is certain that if Patrick had received a mission from the Roman See he would have mentioned it.

According to Muirchu he was raised to the episcopate by Amatorex, a bishop in Gaul (Rolls
Tripartite, p. 273), and was thus consecrated by
a single bishop only (Todd's *St. Patrick*, p. 318).
Certain objections were made on that occasion to
his promotion, which are referred to in his *Confession*
(pp. 58, 59).

There is also no allusion whatever to be found
to any commission received from Rome in the
Hymn composed in honour of his master* during
his lifetime by Secundinus, St. Patrick's own pupil.
In that hymn Patrick is compared to St. Peter and
to St. Paul, and is said to be sent by God like St. Paul
to be an apostle to the Gentiles, and to have been
'advanced by the Saviour for his merits to be a
bishop;' and Secundinus says of Patrick that 'Christ
chose him to be his vicar on the earth.' It is impossible to conceive that in such a eulogy the Roman
commission could have been passed over had it been
actual fact.

Dr. Whitley Stokes observes in reference to that
eulogy: 'The internal evidence of the antiquity of
this hymn is strong. First, the use of the present
tense in describing the saint's actions; secondly, the
absence of all reference to the miracles with which
the *Tripartite* and other Lives are crowded; and
thirdly, the absence of all allusion to the Roman
mission, on which many later writers, from Tirechán
downwards, insist with such persistency' (Rolls
Tripartite, p. cx.).

The hymn ascribed to Fiacc, a contemporary of
St. Patrick, although not written by its reputed

* The original of Secundinus' Hymn is given in Dr. Whitley
Stokes' work, pp. 386–389, with various documents connected
therewith. A good English translation with illustrative notes
is given in Olden's little work, note in our Introduction, p. 23.

author (see Rolls *Tripartite*, p. cxi.), is also silent
on the story of the Roman mission.

The facts connected with Patrick's life which can
be relied on are as follows : Taken captive at sixteen he remained in captivity for about six years
with Milchu somewhere in the valley of the Braid.
On the hill of Slemish he tended cattle and often
poured out prayers to God. He then escaped from
his master, and after many perils recorded in his
Confessio (§§ 7–9) got back to his parents. It is
quite uncertain how he employed the next thirty
years or more, the 'many years' alluded to in his
first paragraph of chap. iii. p. 56. It is also uncertain
what is meant by the second captivity alluded to in
the same paragraph. After two months he regained
his liberty. The reference in § 10 (second paragraph of chap. iii. p. 56) made to a journey through
a desert for twenty-eight days when food failed is
suspiciously like that in § 8, p. 54.

'After a few years' Patrick was again in 'the
Britains' with his parents. What he had been
doing during those years is unknown. But they
seem to have been years of hardships. At this
time he saw the vision, like that of St. Paul at
Troas, which called him to Ireland (p. 57). Dr.
Whitley Stokes' conjectures that some of those thirty
or more years were employed in unsuccessful attempts
to convert the pagan Irish. That, however, is scarcely
probable. He may have spent some of those years
in wandering in other lands, or among 'the islands of
the Tyrrhenian Sea' (as alluded to in the Sayings
given on p. 82). Mr. Newell makes the conjecture
just alluded to.* But, as Newell remarks, Patrick

---

* *St. Patrick: His Life and Teaching*, by E. J. Newell, M.A.
London : Christian Knowledge Society, 1890. A very good
account of St. Patrick and his times is contained in Dr. J. T.

does not appear to have spent that time in studies
as represented by the later legends. He probably
got ordination somewhere during that period, and
after his vision may have gone to Gaul and received
episcopal consecration there, after passing through
the painful ordeal alluded to on pp. 58, 59. But
neither St. Patrick's own writings nor the Hymn of
Secundinus give any account of where he studied or
where he travelled.

It should be noticed, however, that there are evident gaps existing in the *Confession* or autobiography
as it has come down to us. Those gaps may be easily
detected. The first paragraph of chap. iii. p. 56,
comes in awkwardly, however the captivity there
mentioned be explained. There is another gap between the two paragraphs of § 11 on p. 58 of our edition. Another gap appears to exist after the first eight
lines of § 18 on p. 64, for the story of the Scottic
maiden comes in there rather awkwardly. Omis-
sions are, as is admitted, made in quotations from
Scripture (see instances given in notes 17 and 19 on
p. 138). These facts lead to the conclusion that we
have no full account of his life. To attempt to fill
up the gaps from later legends, after the specimens
given of how simple facts have been distorted, is
utterly vain.

Professor Stokes, in his lectures on *Ireland and the
Celtic Church,* has, with great probability, sketched

Fowler's (Vice-Principal of Bishop Hatfield's Hall, Durham),
Introduction to his valuable work, *Adamnavi Vita S. Columbæ,*
edited from Dr. Reeves's text, with an Introduction on early Irish
Church History, notes, and a glossary. Oxford: At the
Clarendon Press, 1894. Dr. Fowler's notes upon the legend of
St. Patrick's driving out the snakes from Ireland, on that of the
shamrock (which is not mentioned earlier than A.D. 1600), and
in reference to the relics of the saint, such as his bell and crozier,
are all interesting.

Patrick's travels in Ireland. Landing at the mouth
of the river Vartry where Wicklow now stands, he
proceeded along the coast until he reached Strangford
Lough, and visited his old master. After some successful missionary expeditions he found it necessary
to confront the heathenism and sun-worship of Ireland at the royal capital, then at Tara, on which
occasion he composed his Irish hymn. The success
which attended that noble endeavour to preach
Christ the true Sun of Righteousness to Loegaire
(the modern Leary), the supreme king of Ireland,
and his court is nowhere alluded to by St. Patrick
himself. It has no doubt been vastly exaggerated
even in the earliest legends. But the blow then delivered at the centre of Irish heathenism soon bore
good fruit, and the poetical beauty and force of the
grand hymn composed on that occasion had no doubt
much to do with that result. Few details are given by
St. Patrick of incidents connected with his missionary labours, and even the earliest records of his
successes, such as that of the conversion of the two
daughters of King Loegaire (given on p. 90 ff.), are
not free from later embellishments. Some idea of
the extent of his missionary travels may be gathered
from the names of places and from traditions freely
scattered over the country, out of which many of
the later legends arose. It may be fairly asserted
that he travelled over a considerable portion of Ireland, always prudently seeking to commence his
work with the conversion of the petty kings and
chieftains of the various parts of the country. He
adhered manfully to the work he had undertaken
amid the difficulties referred to in general terms in
chaps. iv. and v., and seems to have endured much
persecution, even to bonds and imprisonment, as recorded in the close of § 15, p. 62. One imprison-

ment, in which he was put in irons, lasted fourteen
days (p. 62). That he had to suffer grievous wrongs
in the persons of his converts is plain from the
Epistle to Coroticus. When he composed his *Confessio* he was in constant expectation of being reduced to slavery (p. 69), or even laying down his
life by a violent death (p. 70). Martyrdom was,
however, looked forward to without shrinking.
This, however, is sufficient to show that, great as
may have been his missionary successes, Ireland was
very far from having been transformed in his day into
an 'isle of saints.' Hence it should be noted that
St. Patrick's *Vision of the Future* (given on p. 95 ff.),
though probably based on some substratum of fact,
has no doubt been added to in later days.

Dr. Fowler, in his edition of *Adamnan's Life of
Columba* gives the following interesting remarks in
reference to the legend of the expulsion by St.
Patrick of serpents and toads from Ireland, which
appears first in the life written by Jocelin the monk
in the twelfth century. He observes (p. xxxii., note)
that 'Ireland has enjoyed an immunity from snakes
and some other reptiles from time immemorial.
This fact is referred to by Solinus in the third century (*Polyhist.* xxii.), by Bede in the eighth (*Eccl.
Hist.* i. 1), and by many other writers. The subject is fully discussed, with catenæ of quotations
from earlier writers, in Messingham, *Florileg, Insulæ
SS.* (1624), pp. 127–134, and in Colgan, *Tr. Th.*
p. 255.'

Dr. Fowler also has given much important informa-
tion on the eastern origin of Irish Christianity, to
which we would refer the curious reader, for the
subject is too large to be entered into here. It has
also been discussed by Professor G. T. Stokes in
his ninth lecture on *Ireland and the Celtic Church.*

Although the writings of St. Patrick are in the main highly evangelical, it is not strange that Patrick should have imbibed some of the errors which had crept everywhere into the Church of the fifth century. He evidently held 'higher' views with respect to baptism and the Lord's Supper than are set forth in Holy Scripture, while his notions concerning the power committed to the clergy (*Coroticus*, § 3, see our note, p. 144) is certainly objectionable. We are not at the least surprised that a theologian of his age, unacquainted with Hebrew, and knowing only the Scriptures through the medium of some of the old Latin versions, which were based on the old Greek translation, should refer to books of the Apocrypha as inspired Scripture. Though unmarried himself, he has expressed no opinion against a married clergy, and his ancestors for several generations belonged to the clerical ranks. The monks and virgins of his day were not shut up within prison walls like those of a later age. There is no trace in his writings of prayers for the dead, of a belief in a purgatory, of any invocation of saints (see *Confession*, § 9, p. 55, and notes thereon) or of angels, no cultus of the Blessed Virgin, no allusion to any such doctrines as those of transubstantiation, the veneration of sacred images, or so forth. His creed, as set forth in the *Confession* (§ 2, p. 47), is clear and simple. The *Confession of Tours* (see p. 99 ff.), which, if not from his pen, is from that of a pupil of his school, is clear and distinct on the points of absolution, confession to God, and the sole Priesthood of Christ. The Holy Scriptures were ever his sole rule of faith, and the doctrines of grace (though those doctrines were then beginning to be sadly obscured in the Church of the fifth century), are set forth ever and again with humble earnestness.

Hence, though we cannot follow him as a master, perusal of his writings cannot fail to be beneficial to all Christians, and especially to the people of Ireland.

In conclusion of our short memoir of St. Patrick, it may be interesting to append the following Latin hymn in honour of St. Patrick which is found on folio 32 of the Irish MS., *Liber Hymnorum*, in the Library of Trinity College, Dublin. It has been printed (with the exception of the last verse) in Colgan's *Trias Thaum.*, and, I believe, somewhere by Father Hogan. But it is not, however, among the pieces contained in Dr. Whitley Stokes' collection in the second volume of his great work, and Rev. F. E. Warren has again called attention to it in the *Academy* of October 20, 1894. Professor Abbott, of Trinity College, Dublin, has kindly revised it for our purposes. It is interesting, as showing that the author of this very ancient poem was aware of St. Patrick's having been born in Britain, and that he was sent by God to Ireland. It will be noted that no mention is made of any commission received from the Bishop of Rome. We give the poem as in the MS., appending a literal English translation :—

'Incipit ymnus Sancti Patricii.

'Ecce fulget clarissima patricii sollempnitas.
In qua carne deposita felix transcendit sidera.
Qui mox a pueritia diuina plenus gratia
uitam cepit diligere dignitatis angelicae.
Hic felici prosapia natus est in brittania,
perceptoque babtismate studet ad alta tendere.
Sed futurorum prescius clemens et rector dominus
hunc direxit apostolum hiberniae ad populum.

Erat namque haec insola bonis terrae fructifera.
Sed cultore idolatra mergebatur ad infima.
Ad hanc doctor egregius adueniens patricius
predicabat gentilibus quod tenebat operibus.
Confluebat gentilitas ad eius sancta monita.
et respuens diabulum colebat regem omnium.
Gandebatque se liberam remeare ad patriam
qua serpentis astutia ollim expulsa fuerat.
Qua propter, dilectissimi huius in laude presulis.
psallamus christo cordibus alternantes et uocibus.
Ut illius suffragio liberati a uitio.
perfruamur in gloria uisione angelica.
Laus patri sit, et filio, cum spiritu paraclito.
qui suae dono gratiae misertus est hiberniae.

Amen.'

Translation.

(*Here*) *begins the hymn* (*in honour*) *of Saint Patrick.*

Lo ! there shines the most illustrious celebration of
    St. Patrick !
On which he, happy, having laid aside the flesh,
    passed beyond the stars.
Who, full of Divine grace, even from boyhood,
began to love the life of angelic dignity.
He was born in Britain of a noble family,
and having received baptism, he strove to aim at
    high things.
But the Lord, conscious of the future, merciful, and
    ruler,
directed this apostle to the people of Ireland.
For this island was fruitful in the good things of
    the earth
but by its idolatrous worship it was sinking to the
    lowest.

The illustrious doctor, Patrick, coming to this (island),
preached to the Gentiles that which he kept by his works.
The nation flocked to his holy admonitions,
and, rejecting the Devil, worshipped the King of all.
And he rejoiced to return himself to a free country,
from whence the guile of the serpent had been formerly expelled.
Wherefore, dearly beloved, in praise of this leader,
Let us sing to Christ in alternate songs with hearts and voices.
That, freed by his prayers from vice,
We may enjoy the angelic vision in glory.
Praise be to the Father, and the Son, with the Spirit the Comforter,
Who with the gift of his grace pitied Ireland.

Amen.'

The Genuine Writings of Patrick.

I.—THE HYMN, OR 'BREASTPLATE.'

1.

I BIND myself [2] to-day,
    To a strong power, an invocation [3]
        of the Trinity,
    I believe in a Threeness with con-
        fession of a Oneness in [4] the
        Creator of Judgment.[5]

2.

I bind myself to-day,
    To the power [6] of the birth of Christ, with His
      baptism,
    To the power of the crucifixion, with His burial,
    To the power of His resurrection, with His
      ascension,
    To the power of His coming to the judgment of
      doom.

    [1] The figures refer to the notes at the end of the book.

3.

I bind myself to-day,

 To the power of the ranks of cheru- Col. i. 16.
  bim,[7]

 In the obedience of angels, Heb. i. 14.

 In the service of archangels,[8] Rev. xxii. 9.

 In the hope of resurrection unto re- Acts xxiii. 6.
  ward,

 In the prayers of patriarchs,[9] Gen. xxviii. 20.

 In the predictions of prophets, I Pet. i. 12.

 In the preachings of apostles, Matt. xxviii. 19.

 In the faiths of confessors,[10] Acts vii. 55-60. [20]

 In the purity of holy virgins, Rev. xiv. 4.

 In the acts of righteous men. Matt. v. 16.

4.

I bind myself to-day,

 To the power of heaven, Psa. cxlviii. 1.

 The light of sun,

 The brightness of moon,[11] Psa. cxlviii. 3.

 The splendour of fire,

 The speed of lightning,[12] Psa. cxlviii. 7, 8.

 The swiftness of wind, Psa. civ. 4.

 The depth of the sea,

 The stability of earth, Psa. civ. 5.

 The firmness of rocks.[13]

5.

I bind myself to-day,

 To the power of God to guide me, Deut. xxxiii. 27.

 The might of God to uphold me,

 The wisdom of God to teach me, Col. iii. 16.

 The eye of God to watch over me,

 The ear of God to hear me.

1 Pet. iv. 11.

The word of God to speak for me,[14]
The hand of God to protect me,
The way of God to lie before me,[15]

Psa. xviii. 1, 2.

The shield of God to shelter me,

2 Kings vi. 17.

The host of God to defend me,
   Against the snares of demons,
   Against the temptations of vices,

Eph. vi. 10-17.

   Against [the lusts [16]] of nature,
   Against every man who meditates
      injury to me,
   Whether far or near,
   Alone and in a multitude.[17]

6.

I summon to-day [18] around me all these
   powers,
   Against every hostile merciless power

Jude 20.

    directed against my body and my
    soul,

Acts xiii. 8-12.

   Against the incantations of false pro-
    phets,
   Against the black laws of heathenism,
   Against the false laws of heretics,[19]

1 John v. 21.

   Against the deceit of idolatry,
   Against the spells of women, and
    smiths, and Druids,
   Against all knowledge which hath

Jude 10.

    defiled man's body and soul.[20]

7.

Christ protect me to-day,

Mark xvi. 18.

   Against poison, against burning,

Acts xxviii. 22-25.

   Against drowning, against wound,

Heb. x. 35.

That I may receive a multitude of
   rewards.

8.

Christ with me, Christ before me,
Christ behind me, Christ within me,
Christ beneath me, Christ above me,
Christ at my right, Christ at my left,
Christ in breadth, Christ in length,   Eph. iii. 18, 19.
   Christ in height.[21]

9.

Christ in the heart of every man who
   thinks of me,
Christ in the mouth of every man who
   speaks to me,
Christ in the eye of every man that sees
   me,
Christ in the ear of every man that
   hears me.

10.

I bind myself to-day,
   To a strong power, an invocation of
     the Trinity,
   I believe in a Threeness with con-
     fession of a Oneness in the Creator
     of Judgment.[22]

11.

Salvation is the Lord's,   Psa. iii. 8.
Salvation is the Lord's,
Salvation is Christ's,   Rev. vii. 10.
Let Thy salvation, O Lord, be ever   Isa. xxv. 9.
   with us.[23]

II.—THE CONFESSION OF PATRICK.

THE BEGINNING OF THE BOOKS OF SAINT PATRICK, BISHOP.[1]

CHAPTER I.

*Patrick's birth and parentage—Patrick a Briton—His captivity—
The cause of his writing a desire to praise God for His benefits
—His creed—His modesty, and want of learning—Raised u
by God to do His work.*

PATRICK,[2] a sinner, the rudest and the least of all the faithful, and most contemptible to very many, had for my father Calpornius, a deacon, a son of Potitus [3] a presbyter,[4] who dwelt in the village of Bannavem [5] Taberniæ,[6] for he had a small farm [7] hard by the place where I was taken captive.[8] I was then nearly sixteen years of age. I did not

[1] The figures in the text refer to the notes at the end of the book.

46

know the true God ; [9] and I was taken to Ireland in captivity with so many thousand men, in accordance with our deserts, because we departed from God, and we kept not His precepts, and were not obedient to our priests, [10] who admonished us for our salvation.

And the Lord brought down upon us 'the wrath of His indignation,' * [11] and dispersed us among many nations, [12] even to the end of the earth, where now my littleness [13] is seen among foreigners. And there the Lord opened (to me) the sense of my unbelief, [14] that, though late, I might remember my sins, and that I might return with [15] my whole heart to the Lord my God, who had respect to my humiliation, and pitied my youth and ignorance, [16] and took care of me before I knew Him, and before I had wisdom, or could discern between good and evil ; and protected [17] me and comforted me as a father does a son.

2. Wherefore I cannot keep silent—nor is it indeed expedient (to do so)—concerning such great benefits, and such great favour as the Lord has vouchsafed to me in the land of my captivity ; because this is our recompense (to Him) that after our chastening, or knowledge of God, we should exalt and confess His wonderful works † [18] before every nation which is under the whole heaven.

Because there is no other God, neither ever was, neither before, nor shall be hereafter, except God the Father, unbegotten, [19] without beginning. From whom is all beginning ; upholding all things, as we say ; and His Son Jesus Christ, whom indeed with the Father, we testify to have always been, before the origin of the world, spiritually with the Father ;

* 2 Chron. xxix. 10.   † Psa. cvii. 15.

in an inexplicable [20] manner begotten before all beginning; and by Himself were made the things visible and invisible;[21] made man; (and), death having been vanquished, received into the heavens to the Father.* [22] And He has given to Him all power 'above every name of those that are in heaven, on earth, and under the earth,[23] that every tongue should confess' † to Him [24] that Jesus Christ is Lord and God, in whom we believe, and expect (His) coming, to be ere long; 'the Judge of the living and of the dead,' ‡ 'who will render to every one according to his deeds.' § [25] And He hath 'poured upon us abundantly' ‖ the Holy Spirit, a gift and pledge of immortality; [26] who makes the faithful and obedient to become 'sons of God,[27] and joint-heirs with Christ'; ¶ whom we confess and adore —one God in the Holy Trinity of the sacred name.[28]

For He Himself has said by the prophet, 'Call upon Me in the day of thy tribulation, and I will deliver thee, and thou shalt magnify Me.' ** [29] And again He saith, 'It is honourable to reveal and confess the works of God.' †† [30]

3. Although I am in many respects imperfect, I wish my brethren and acquaintances to know my disposition,[31] and that they may be able to comprehend the wish of my soul. I am not ignorant of the testimony of my Lord, who witnesses in the Psalm, 'Thou shalt destroy those that speak a lie.' ‡‡ [32] And again, 'The mouth that belieth killeth the soul.' §§ And the same Lord says in the Gospel,[33] 'The idle word that men shall speak, they

---

* Rev. iii. 21.   † Phil. ii. 9–11.   ‡ Acts x. 42.
§ Rom. ii. 6.   ‖ Titus iii. 6.   ¶ Rom. viii. 17.
** Psa. l. 15.   †† Tobit xii. 7.   ‡‡ Psa. v. 6.
§§ Wisdom i. 11.

shall render an account for it in the day of judgment.' * 34 Therefore, I ought earnestly with fear
and trembling to dread this sentence in that day
when no one shall be able to withdraw himself, or
to hide, but when we all together shall render
account of even the smallest of our sins before the
tribunal of the Lord Christ.35

Wherefore, I thought of writing long ago, but
hesitated even till now; because I feared falling
into the tongue of men ; 36 because I have not
learned like others who have drunk in, in the best
manner, both law and sacred literature in both ways
equally ; 37 and have never changed their language
from infancy, but have always added more to its
perfection. For my language and speech is translated into a foreign tongue.38

4. As can be easily proved from the drivel 39 of
my writing—how I have been instructed and learned
in diction ; 40 because the wise man says : 'For by
the tongue is discerned understanding and knowledge, and the teaching of truth.'† 41 But what
avails an excuse [although] according to truth,
especially when accompanied with presumption ? 42
Since indeed I myself, now in my old age, strive
after what I did not learn in my youth, because
they prevented 43 me from learning thoroughly that
which I had read through before. But who believes
me, although I should say as I have already said ?
When a youth, nay almost a boy in words,44 I was
taken captive, before I knew what I ought to seek,
or what I ought to aim at,45 or what I ought to
avoid. Hence I blush to-day, and greatly fear to
expose my unskilfulness, because, not being eloquent,46 I cannot express myself with clearness
and brevity, nor even as the spirit moves, and

* Matt. xii. 36.   † Ecclus. iv. 29.

the mind and endowed understanding point out.[47]

But if it had been granted to me even as to others, I would not, however, be silent, because of the recompense. And if, perhaps, it appears to some, that I put myself forward in this matter with my ignorance and slower tongue, it is, however, written : 'Stammering tongues shall learn quickly to speak peace.' * [48] How much more ought we to aim at this—we who are the 'epistle of Christ'—for salvation even to the end of the earth,†—and ir not eloquent, yet powerful and very strong—written in your hearts 'not with ink,' it is testified, . . . 'but by the Spirit of the living God.' ‡ [49]

5. And again the Spirit testifies ; 'and husbandry was ordained by the Most High.' § [50] Therefore, I, first a rustic, a fugitive, unlearned, indeed, not knowing how to provide for the future—but I know this most certainly, that before I was humbled I was like a stone lying in deep mud ; and He who is mighty came, and in His own mercy raised me, and lifted me up, and placed me on the top of the wall. ‖ [51] And hence I ought loudly to cry out, to return also something to the Lord for His so great benefits, here and in eternity, which (benefits) the mind of men cannot estimate. But, therefore, be ye astonished, both great and small, who fear God. And ye rhetoricians, who do not know the Lord,[52] hear and examine : Who aroused me, a fool, from the midst of those who appear to be wise, and skilled in the laws, and powerful in speech and in every matter ? And me—who am detested by this world—He has inspired me beyond others (if indeed I be such), but on condition that with fear and

* Isa. xxxii. 4.   † Acts xiii. 47.   ‡ 2 Cor. iii. 3.
§ Ecclus. vii. 15.   ‖ Comp. 1 Peter ii. 5 ; Eph. ii. 21, 22.

reverence, and without complaining, I should faithfully serve [53] the nation—to which the love of
Christ has transferred me, and given me for my life
—if I should be worthy [54]—that, in fine, I should
serve them with humility and in truth.[55]

[N.B.—The Rev. Professor Abbott, of Trinity
College, Dublin, has kindly collated the Dublin MS.
for me.]

CHAPTER II.

*Patrick's desire to recount God's mercies—Employed in feeding cattle
—Earnestness in prayer—Promised deliverance in a dream—
His escape from slavery—Arrival at the ship—Refused a
passage—Betakes himself to prayer—Admitted on board—
Desires to convert the sailors—Journey in the desert—Wonder-
ful deliverance from perishing by hunger—Result of prayer—
Refuses food offered to idols—Conflict with Satan—Calls on
'Helias' for deliverance.*

N the measure,[1] therefore of the faith,* of the Trinity it behoves me to distinguish, without shrinking from danger, to make known the gift of God, and His 'everlasting consolation,'† and without fear to spread faithfully everywhere the name of God, in order that even after my death I may leave it as a bequest[2] to my brethren, and to my sons, whom I have baptized in the Lord—so many thousand men. And I was not worthy nor deserving that the Lord should grant this to His servant ; that after going through afflictions and so many difficulties,[2b] after captivity, after many years, He should grant me so great favour among that

* Rom. xii. 3.   † 2 Thess. ii. 16.

nation, which when I was yet in my youth I never hoped for, nor thought of.

But after I had come to Ireland I daily used to feed cattle,[3] and I prayed frequently during the day ;[4] the love of God and the fear of Him increased more and more, and faith became stronger, and the spirit was stirred ; so that in one day I said about a hundred prayers, and in the night nearly the same ; so that I used even to remain in the woods and in the mountain ; before daylight I used to rise to prayer, through snow, through frost, through rain, and felt no harm ; nor was there any slothfulness in me, as I now perceive, because the spirit was then fervent within me.

And there indeed one night, in my sleep, I heard a voice saying to me, ' Thou fastest well [fasting so], thou shalt soon go to thy country.' And again, after a very short time, I heard a response saying to me, ' Behold, thy ship is ready.'[5] And it was not near, but perhaps two hundred miles away, and I never had been there, nor was I acquainted with any of the men there.

7. After this I took flight, and left the man[6] with whom I had been six years ;[7] and I came in the strength of the Lord, who directed my way for good ;[8] and I feared nothing till I arrived at that ship. And on that same day on which I arrived, the ship moved out of its place, and I asked them (the sailors) that I might go away and sail with them.[9] And it displeased the captain, and he answered sharply with indignation,[10] ' Do not by any means seek to go with us.' And when I heard this, I separated myself from them in order to go to the hut where I lodged. And on the way I began to pray ; and before I had ended my prayer I heard one of them, and he was calling loudly after me, ' Come quickly, for these men are calling you.'

And immediately I returned to them, and they
began to say to me, 'Come, for we receive you in
good faith,[11] make friendship with us in whatever
way you wish.' And in that day I accordingly dis-
dained to make friendship with them,[12] on account
of the fear of God. But in very deed I hoped of
them that they would come into the faith of Jesus
Christ, because they were heathen, and on account
of this I clave to them.[13] And we sailed immediately.[14]

8. After three days we reached land, and for
twenty-eight [15] days we made our journey through
a desert. And food failed them, and hunger prevailed over them. And one day the captain began
to say to me, 'What (is it), O Christian? You say
thy God is great and almighty; why, therefore,
canst thou not pray for us, for we are perishing
with hunger? [16] For it will be a difficult matter for
us ever again to see any human being.' But I said
to them plainly, 'Turn with faith [17] to the Lord
my God, to whom nothing is impossible, that He
may send food this day [18] for us in your path, even
till you are satisfied,[19] for it abounds everywhere
with Him.' And God assisting, it so came to pass.
Behold, a herd of swine appeared in the path before
our eyes, and (my companions) killed many of them,
and remained there two nights, much refreshed.
And their dogs were filled, for many of them had
fainted [20] and were left half-dead along the way.
And after that they gave the greatest thanks to God,
and I was honoured in their eyes.

9. From that day forth they had food in abundance.[21] They also found wild honey, and offered
me a part of it. And one of them said, 'It has
been offered in sacrifice.' Thanks to God! I
consequently tasted none of it.[22] But the same

night while I was sleeping, and Satan greatly tempted me, in a way which I shall remember as long as I am in this body. And he fell upon me [23] like a huge rock, and I had no power in my limbs, save that [24] it came to me, into my mind, that I should call out 'Helias.' [25] And in that moment I saw the sun rise in the heaven; and while I was crying out 'Helias' [26] with all my might, behold the splendour of that sun fell upon me, and at once removed the weight from me. And I believe I was aided by Christ my Lord, and His Spirit was then crying out for me, [27] and I hope likewise that it will be thus in the days of my oppression, as the Lord says in the Gospel, 'It is not you that speak, but the Spirit of your Father, which speaketh in you.' * [28]

* Matt. x. 20.

CHAPTER III.

Second captivity—Deliverance—Return to Britain—Called in a vision of the night to Ireland—The Spirit praying in him—Charge brought against him by his seniors—Cause of the charge—Vision of 'the writing against him'—The Lord on his side—Inconsistent conduct of a friend—Patrick returns thanks to God—Made a missionary by the grace of Christ.

AND again, after many years, I was taken captive once more.[1] On that first night, therefore, I remained with them. But I heard a Divine response saying to me,[2] 'But for two months thou shalt be with them;' which accordingly came to pass. On that sixtieth night the Lord delivered me out of their hands.

Even on our journey He provided for us food and fire, and dry weather every day, till on the fourteenth day we all arrived.[3] As I stated before, we pursued our journey for twenty-eight days through the desert, and the very night on which we all arrived [4] we had no food left.[5]

And again, after a few years, I was in the Britains [6] with my parents, who received me as a son, and

earnestly besought me that, now at least, after the
many hardships I had endured, I would never leave
them again. And there I saw, indeed, in the bosom
of the night, a man coming as it were from Ireland,
Victoricus by name, with innumerable letters, and he
gave one of them to me. And I read the beginning
of the letter containing 'The Voice of the Irish.'
And while I was reading aloud the beginning of the
letter, I myself thought indeed in my mind that I
heard the voice of those who were near the wood of
Foclut,[7] which is close by the Western Sea. And
they cried out thus as if with one voice,[8] 'We entreat thee, holy youth, that thou come, and hence-
forth walk among us.' And I was deeply moved in
heart, and could read no further ; and so I awoke.
Thanks be to God, that after very many years the
Lord granted to them according to their cry !

11. And on another night, I know not, God
knows, whether in me, or near me, with most
eloquent words which I heard, and could not
understand,[9] except at the end of the speech one
spoke as follows, 'He who gave His life for thee *
is He who speaks in thee ;' [10] and so I awoke full of
joy.[11] And again I saw Him praying in me,[12] and
He was [13] as it were within my body, and I heard
above me,[14] that is, above the inner man,[15] and there
He was praying mightily with groanings. And mean-
while I was stupefied and astonished, and pondered
who it could be that was praying in me. But at the
end of the prayer He so spoke as if He were the
Spirit.[16] And so I awoke, and remembered that the
Apostle says, 'The Spirit helps the infirmities of our
prayers. For we know not what we should pray for
as we ought ; but the Spirit Himself asketh for
us with unspeakable groanings,'† [17] which cannot

* 1 John iii. 16.　　　　　† Rom. viii. 26.

be expressed [18] in words. And again, (he says)
'The Lord is our advocate, and prays for us." * [19]

[And when I was harassed by some of my seniors
who came, and (urged) my sins against my laborious
episcopate, so that on that day I was strongly driven
to fall away, here and for ever. But the Lord spared
a proselyte and stranger for His name's sake. He
kindly and mightily aided me in this treading-under,
because in the stain and disgrace I did not come out
badly. I pray God that it be not reckoned to them
as an occasion of sin. For after thirty years they
found me, and brought against me a word which I
had confessed before I was a deacon.[20]

12. Under anxiety, with a troubled mind, I
told my most intimate friend what I had one day
done in my boyhood, nay in one hour; because I
was not then used to overcome.[21] I know not, God
knows, whether I was then fifteen years of age; and
I did not believe in the one God from my infancy;
but I remained in death and unbelief until I was
severely chastised; and in truth I have been
humbled by hunger and nakedness, and that daily.
On the other hand,[22] I did not of my own accord
go to Ireland until I was almost worn out. But this
was rather good for me; [23] for by this I was corrected
by the Lord—and He fitted me that I should be
to-day what formerly was far from me; that I
should be filled with care, and be concerned for
the salvation of others; since at that time I did
not think even about myself.

Then in that day on which I was reproached for
the things above-mentioned; [24] on that night,] I saw
in a vision of the night, a writing against me,[25]
without honour. And at the same time I heard
a response [26] saying to me, 'We have seen [27] with

* 1 John ii. 1 ; Rom. viii. 34.

displeasure the face of the designate [28] with his name stripped.' He did not say, 'Thou hast seen with displeasure,' but 'We have seen with displeasure,' as if He had joined Himself to me, as He has said, 'He that toucheth you is as he that toucheth the apple of Mine eye.'* [29]   Therefore I give thanks to Him, who comforted me in all things, that He did not hinder me from the journey on which I had resolved, and also from my work which I had learned of Christ my Lord. But the more from that (time) I felt in myself [30] no little power, and my faith was approved before God and men.

13. But on this account I boldly assert that my conscience does not reprove me now or for the future.[31] 'God is my witness'† that I have not lied in those things I have related. [But [32] I am the more sorry for my very dear friend—to whom I trusted even my life—that we should have deserved to hear such a response. And I ascertained from several brethren before that defence [33] that, when I was not present, nor in the Britains,[34] nor did it originate with me—even he in my absence made a fight for me.[35] Even he had said to me with his own mouth, 'Behold, thou art to be promoted to the rank of bishop,'—of which I was not worthy. But whence then did it occur to him afterwards that before all, good and bad, he should publicly put discredit upon me, although he had before of his own accord gladly conceded (that honour to me)? It is the Lord, who is greater than all.

I have said enough. But, however, I ought not to hide the gift of God which He bestowed upon us in the land of my captivity. For then I earnestly sought Him, and there I found Him, and He pre-

* Zech. ii. 8.
† Rom. i. 9 ; comp. Gal. i. 20 ; 2 Cor. i. 23.

served me from all iniquities, so I believe, because of His Spirit 'that dwelleth in (me),' * which has wrought in me again boldly 35[b] even to this day. But God knows, if a man had spoken this to me, I might have been silent for the love of Christ.

14. Wherefore, I give unwearied thanks to my God, who has kept me faithful in the day of my temptation ; so that I may to-day confidently offer to Him my soul—to Christ my Lord—as a sacrifice, 'a living victim ;' † 36 who saved me from all my difficulties, ‡ so that I may say : 'Who am I, Lord ?' § 37 and what is my vocation,‖ 38 that to me Thou hast co-operated by such Divine grace with me ! 39 So that to-day I can constantly rejoice among the Gentiles 40 and magnify ¶ 41 Thy name wherever I may be, not only in prosperity, but also in distresses ; ** that whatever may happen to me, whether good or evil, I ought to receive it equally, and always to give thanks to God, who has shown me that I should believe in Him, the indubitable one, 42 without ceasing, and that He will hear me ; 43 and that I, though ignorant, may in these last days attempt to approach this work, so pious and so wonderful ; that I may imitate some of those of whom before the Lord long ago predicted (that they) should preach His Gospel, ' for a testimony to all nations ' †† 44 before the end of the world. Which, therefore, has been so fulfilled, as we have seen. Behold, we are witnesses that the Gospel has been preached everywhere, in places where there is no man beyond. 45]

* Rom. viii. 11.   † Rom. xii. 1.   ‡ Psa. xxxiv. 7.
§ 2 Sam. vii. 18.   ‖ 1 Cor. i. 26.   ¶ Rom. xv. 9.
      ** 2 Cor. xii. 9, 10.   †† Matt. xxiv. 14.

CHAPTER IV.

Patrick's labours and deliverances—Temptations to remain at home—
Willingness to die for Christ—The work accomplished by God's
grace—The duty of missionary work—Results of his mission in
Ireland—His resolve to continue in the mission-field, and his
reliance on God.

BUT it would be long to relate all my labour, in details, or even in part. Briefly, I may tell how the most holy [1] God often delivered me from slavery, and from twelve dangers [2] by which my life was imperilled, besides many snares, and things which I cannot express in words, neither would I give trouble to my readers. But there is God the Author (of all), who knew all things before they came to pass.

[3 So, however, the Divine response very frequently admonished me His poor pupil.[4] Whence (came) this wisdom to me, which was not in me, I who neither knew the number of my days,* [5] nor was acquainted with God ? Whence (came) to me afterwards the gift so great, so beneficial, to know God, or to love Him, that I should leave country and parents, and

* Psa. xxxix. 4.

61

many gifts which were offered to me with weeping
and tears? And, moreover, I offended against my
wish certain of my seniors. But, God overruling,
I by no means consented or complied with them.
It was not my grace *[6] but God who conquered in
me,[7] and resisted them all; so that I came to the
Irish peoples, to preach the Gospel, and to suffer
insults from unbelievers; that I should listen to
reproach about my wandering,[8] and (endure) many
persecutions, even to chains; and that I should
give up my noble birth [9] for the benefit of others.

16. And if I be worthy, I am ready to lay down
my life unhesitatingly, and most gladly for His
name; and there I wish to spend it, even till death,
if the Lord permit.][10]

For I am greatly a debtor to the God who has
bestowed on me such grace, that many people
through me should be born again to God,[11] and that
everywhere clergy should be ordained for a people
newly coming to the faith, whom the Lord took
from the ends of the earth, as He had promised of
old by His prophets: 'To Thee the Gentiles will
come and say, As our fathers made false idols, and
there is no profit in them.' †[12]   And again: 'I have
set Thee to be the light of the Gentiles, that Thou
mayest be for salvation unto the utmost part of the
earth.'‡[13]   And there I am willing to await the
promise of Him who never fails, as He promises in
the Gospel: 'They shall come from the east and
the west, and shall sit down with Abraham, and
Isaac, and Jacob;'§[14] as we believe that believers
shall come from all the world.[15]

17. Therefore it becomes us to fish well and
diligently, as the Lord premonishes and teaches,

* 1 Cor. xv. 10.   † Jer. xvi. 19.
‡ Acts xiii. 47; Isa. xlix. 6.   § Matt. viii. 11.

saying : 'Come ye after Me, and I will make you
fishers of men.'* And again He says by the prophets : 'Behold I send many fishers and hunters,
saith the Lord.'† [16] Therefore it is very necessary
to spread our nets, so that a copious multitude
and crowd may be taken for God, and that everywhere there may be clergy, who shall baptize and
exhort a people needy and anxious, as the Lord
admonishes and teaches in the Gospel, saying :
'Going, therefore, teach ye all nations, baptizing
them in the name of the Father, and of the
Son, and of the Holy Ghost, teaching them to
observe all things whatsoever I have commanded
you : and behold I am with you all days, even to
the consummation of the world.' ‡ [17] And again :
'Going, therefore, into the whole world, preach
the Gospel to every creature. He that believeth
and is baptized shall be saved, but he that believeth
not shall be condemned.' § [18] [And again : 'This
Gospel of the kingdom shall be preached in the
whole world, for a testimony to all nations, and then
shall the consummation come.'‖ [19] And also the
Lord, foretelling by the prophet, says : 'And it
shall be in the last days, saith the Lord, I will pour
out of My Spirit upon all flesh, and your sons and
your daughters shall prophesy, and your sons shall
see visions, [20] and your old men shall dream dreams.
And upon My servants indeed and upon My handmaids I will pour out in those days of My Spirit,
and they shall prophesy.'¶ And in Osee He says :
'I will call that which was not My people My
people . . . and her who had not obtained mercy ;
and it shall be in the place where it was said, You

---

* Matt. iv. 19.   † Jer. xvi. 16.
‡ Matt. xxviii. 19, 20.   § Mark xvi. 15, 16.
‖ Matt. xxiv. 14.   ¶ Acts ii. 17, 18 ; Joel ii. 28, 29.

are not My people, there they shall be called the
sons of the living God.' * 21

18. Whence, then, has it come to pass that in
Ireland 22 they who never had any knowledge, and
until now have only worshipped idols and unclean
things, have lately become a people of the Lord, and
are called the sons of God? Sons of the Scots 23
and daughters of chieftains are seen to be monks and
virgins 24 of Christ. 25 [And there was even one
blessed Scottic maiden, nobly-born, very beautiful,
of adult age, whom I baptized. And after a few
days she came to us for a reason, 26 and intimated to
us that she had received a response from a messenger
of God, 27 and he advised her that she should be a
virgin of Christ, and that she should draw near her-
self to God. 28 Thanks be to God! On the sixth
day after that, she most excellently and eagerly
seized on that 29 which also all the virgins of God
do; not with the will of their fathers—but they
suffer persecution and false reproaches from their
parents; and notwithstanding the number increases
the more; and of our own race 30 who were born
there (there are those), we know not the number,
besides widows and those who are continent.
But those (women) who are detained in slavery
especially suffer; in spite of terrors and threats, they
have assiduously persevered. But the Lord gave grace
to many of my handmaids, for, although they are
forbidden, they zealously imitate Him.

19. Wherefore, though I could wish to leave
them, and had been most willingly prepared to pro-
ceed to the Britains, as to my country and parents;
and not that only, but even (to go) as far as to the
Gauls, to visit the brethren and to see the face of
the saints of my Lord. God knows that I greatly

---

* Hosea i. 9, 10; Rom. ix. 25, 26.

desired it.   But I am 'bound in the Spirit,'* who
'witnesseth to me,'† that if I should do this, He
would hold me guilty ; and I fear to lose the labour
which I have commenced ; and not I, but Christ
the Lord, who commanded me to come, and be with
them for the rest of my life.   If the Lord will,‡
and if He will keep me from every evil way,§ [31] that
I may not sin before Him.   But I hope (to do) that
which I ought ; but I trust not myself, so long as I
am in 'this body of death ;'‖ for strong is he who
daily tries to subvert me from the faith,[32] and from
the chastity of religion proposed (to myself), not
feignedly (which I will observe), even to the end
of my life, to Christ my Lord.   But the flesh,
which is in enmity, ¶ [33] always leads to death, that is,
to unlawful desires to be unlawfully gratified.   And
I know in part that I have not led a perfect life,[34]
as other believers.   But I confess to my Lord, and
I do not blush before Him, because I lie not : from
the time that I knew Him in my youth, the love
of God and His fear have increased in me ; and
until now, by the favour of the Lord, 'I have kept
the faith.' ** [35]

* Acts xx. 22.   † Acts xx. 23.   ‡ James iv. 15.
§ 2 Tim. iv. 18 ; comp. Gen. xxviii. 20.
‖ Rom. vii. 24.   ¶ Rom. viii. 7.   ** 2 Tim. iv. 8.

CHAPTER V.

Patrick's boldness in writing—God's mercy to him in spite of the reproach of men—His desire that others should do more for Christ —His despisal of riches—Did not preach or administer sacraments or orders for gain—His trials in the exercise of his mission—He rejoices in his expenditure and sufferings for Christ—His longing for martyrdom—His belief in the Resurrection—His denunciation of Sun-worship—His final protestation—What he effected was all by God's grace.

LET him who will laugh and insult, I will not be silent, nor will I hide the signs and wonders which were ministered to me by the Lord, many years before they came to pass, as He who knew all things even before the world began.*[1]

But hence I ought to give thanks without ceasing to God,† who often pardoned my ignorance (and) my negligence,[2] even out of place, not in one instance only—so that He was not fiercely angry with me, as being one who was permitted to be His helper. And

---

* Acts xv. 18.   † Comp. 1 Thess. v. 17, 18.

66

yet I did not immediately yield to what was pointed
out to me, and (to) what the Spirit suggested. And
the Lord had pity on me among thousands of
thousands,[3] because He saw in me that I was ready,
but that in my case for these (reasons) I knew
not what to do about my position; because many
were hindering this mission, and already were
talking among themselves, and saying behind my
back, 'Why does that fellow put himself into
danger among enemies who know not God?' Not
(as though they spoke) for the sake of malice, but
because it was not a wise thing in their opinion,
as I myself also testify, on account of my defect
in learning.[4] And I did not readily recognise the
grace that was then in me; but now I know that I
ought before[5] [to have been obedient to God calling
me].

21. Now, therefore, I have related simply, to my
brethren and fellow-servants who have believed me,
(the reason) why I have preached and do preach, in
order to strengthen and confirm your faith. Would
that you might aim at greater, and perform mightier
things![6] This will be my glory, because 'a wise
son is the glory of a father.'*[7]

You know, and God also, how I have conducted
myself among you from my youth, both in the faith
of the truth, and in sincerity of heart.†[8] Even in
the case of those nations among whom I dwell, I
have always kept faith with them, and I will keep
it.[9] God knows I have over-reached none of them;
neither do I think of it, [that is, of acting thus] on
account of God and His Church, lest I should excite
persecution against them and us all, and lest through
me the name of the Lord should be blasphemed;

---

* Prov. x. 1; xv. 20.　　　　† 1 Thess. ii. 10.

because it is written, 'Woe to the man through whom the name of the Lord is blasphemed.'*[10] For though I am unskilful in names,[11] yet I have endeavoured in some respects to serve even my Christian brethren, and the virgins of Christ, and religious women, who have given to me small voluntary gifts,[12] and have cast off some of their ornaments upon the altar; and I used to return these to them; although they were offended with me because I did so. But I (did it) for the hope of eternal life, in order to keep myself prudently in everything, so that the unbelieving may not catch me on any pretext, or the ministry of my service; and that, even in the smallest point, I might not give the unbelievers an occasion to defame or depreciate (me).†

22. But perhaps, since I have baptized so many thousand men, I might have expected half a screpall[12b] from some of them? Tell it to me, and I will restore it to you.‡ Or when the Lord ordained everywhere clergy, through my humble ministry, I dispensed the rite (Lat. *ministerium*) gratuitously. If I asked of any of them even the price of my shoe, tell it against me, and I will restore you more. I spent for you, that they might receive me; and among you, and everywhere, I travelled for your sake, amid many perils, even to remote places, where there was no one beyond, and where no one else had ever penetrated—to baptize or ordain clergy, or to confirm the people. The Lord granting it, I diligently and most cheerfully, for your salvation, defrayed all things. During this time I gave presents to the kings[13]; besides which I gave pay to their sons who escorted me; and nevertheless they seized

---

* Lev. xxiv. 16; Rom. ii. 24.   † Comp. 2 Cor. vi. 3 ff.
‡ 1 Sam. xii. 3.

me,[14] together with my companions. And on that day they eagerly desired to kill me; but the time had not yet come.* And they seized all things that they found with us, and they also bound me with iron. And on the fourteenth day the Lord set me free from their power; and whatever was ours was restored to us, for God's sake, and the attached friends whom we had before provided.

23. But you know how much I paid to those who acted as judges [15] throughout all the regions which I more frequently visited. For I think that I distributed among them not less than the hire of fifteen men.[16] So that you might enjoy me, and I may always enjoy you in the Lord, I do not regret it, nor is it enough for me—I still 'spend, and will spend for your souls.'[17]] God is mighty, and may He grant to me that in future I may spend myself for your souls.[18] Behold, 'I call God to witness upon my soul'† 'that I lie not';‡ neither that you may have occasion, nor because I hope for honour from any man.[19] Sufficient to me is honour which is not belied.[20] But I see that now I am exalted by the Lord above measure§ [21] in the present age; and I was not worthy, nor deserving that He should aid me in this; since I know that poverty and calamity suit me better than riches and luxuries. But Christ the Lord was poor for us.||

But I, poor and miserable, even if I wished for riches, yet have them not, 'neither do I judge my own self;'¶ [22] because I daily expect either murder, or to be circumvented, or to be reduced to slavery, or mishap of some kind. [But[23] 'I fear none of these things,'** [24] on account of the promises of the

---

* John viii. 20.   † 2 Cor. i. 23.   ‡ Gal. i. 20.
§ 2 Cor. xii. 7. || 2 Cor. viii. 9.   ¶ 1 Cor. iv. 3.
** Rev. ii. 10.

heavens ; for I have cast myself into the hands of
the Omnipotent God, who [25] rules everywhere, as
saith the prophet, 'Cast thy thought on the Lord,
and He will sustain thee.' * [26]

24. Behold now, I commend my soul to my most
faithful God, † for whom I discharge an embassage
in my ignoble condition, because indeed He does not
accept the person, ‡ [27] and He chose me to this office,
that I might be one of the least of His ministers.
But 'what shall I render Him for all the things that
He hath rendered to me ? § [28]   But what shall I say,
or what shall I promise to my Lord ?   Because I
have no power, [29] unless He had given it to me, but
He searches 'the heart and reins ;' ‖ because I desire
enough and too much, and am prepared that He
should give me 'to drink of His cup,' as He has
granted to others that love Him. ¶

Wherefore may it never happen to me from my
Lord, to lose His people, (people) whom He has
gained in the utmost parts of the earth. [30]   I pray
God that He may give me perseverance, and count
me worthy to render myself a faithful witness to Him,
even till my departure, on account of my God.   And
if I have ever imitated anything good on account of
my God, whom I love, I pray Him to grant me, that
with those proselytes and captives, I may pour out
my blood for His name's sake, even although I myself
may even be deprived of burial, and my corpse most
miserably be torn limb from limb by dogs, or by wild
beasts, or that the fowls of heaven should devour it.
I believe most certainly that if this should happen
to me, I shall have gained both soul and body. [31]

---

* Psa. lv. 22.   † 1 Pet. iv. 19.
‡ Gal. ii. 6 ; Prov. xviii. 5.   § Psa. cxvi. 12.
‖ Psa. vii. 9 ; Jer. xi. 20.   ¶ Matt. xx. 22, 23.

Because without any doubt we shall rise in that day in the brightness of the sun, that is, in the glory of Jesus Christ, our Redeemer, as 'sons of the living God,'*[32] and 'joint-heirs with Christ,'† and to be 'conformable to His image;'‡ for 'of Him, and through Him, and in Him'§ we shall reign.[33]

25. For that sun which we behold, at God's command, rises daily for us—but it shall never reign, nor shall its splendour continue;[34] but all even that worship it, miserable beings, shall wretchedly come to punishment.[35] But we who believe in and adore the true sun,[36] Jesus Christ, who will never perish;[37] neither shall he 'who does His will'—but 'shall continue for ever,'||—as Christ continues for ever,[38] who reigns with God the Father Almighty, and with the Holy Spirit, before the ages, and now, and through all the ages of ages. Amen.

Behold, I will, again and again, declare briefly the words of my Confession. I testify in truth, and in joy of heart, before God and His holy angels, ¶[39] that I never had any reason, except the Gospel and its promises, for ever returning to that people from whom I had formerly escaped with difficulty.][40]

But I beg of those who believe and fear God, whoever shall deign to look into or receive this writing, which Patrick the sinner, unlearned indeed, has written in Ireland, that no one may ever say, if I have done or demonstrated anything according to the will of God,[41] however little, that it was my ignorance (which did it); but judge ye, and let it

---

* Hosea i. 10. † Rom. viii. 17.
‡ Rom. viii. 29. § Rom. xi. 36.
|| 1 John ii. 17. ¶ 1 Tim. v. 21.

be most truly believed, that it has been the gift of
God.   And this is my Confession before I die.

*Thus far the volume which Patrick wrote with his
own hand : On the seventeenth of March, Patrick was
translated to heaven.*[42]

III.—THE EPISTLE TO COROTICUS.[1]

PATRICK, a sinner, unlearned, declare indeed that I have been appointed a bishop in Ireland ; I most certainly believe that from God I have received what I am. I dwell thus among barbarians,* a proselyte and an exile, on account of the love of God. He is witness that it is so. Not because I desired to pour out anything from my mouth so harsh and severe, but I am compelled, stirred up by zeal for God and for the truth of Christ, for the love of my neighbours and sons, for whom I have abandoned country and parents, and my soul, even unto death, if I be worthy (of such honour). I have vowed to my God to teach the nations, although I be despised by some.

With my own hand I have written and composed these words, to be given and handed to the soldiers,

---

* Lat. *inter barbaras*, which must either be corrected into *barbaros*, as we have done, or the word gentes, *nations*, supplied, as by Dr. W. Stokes.

---

to be sent to Coroticus;[2] I do not say, to my
fellow-citizens, and to the citizens of the Roman
saints, but to the citizens of demons, on account of
their own evil deeds, who by hostile practice of
barbarians live in death;[3]—companions of the Scots
and apostate Picts[4]—who stain themselves bloody
with the blood of innocent Christians, whom I have
begotten without number to God, and have confirmed in Christ.

2. On the day after that in which (these Christians) were anointed neophytes in white robes, while
it (the anointing) was yet glistening on their fore-
heads—they were cruelly massacred and slaughtered
with the sword by those above-mentioned.[5] And I
sent a letter with a holy presbyter, whom I taught
from his infancy, with (other) clergy (begging them)
that they would restore to us some of the plunder,
or of the baptized captives whom they took, (but)
they mocked at them. Therefore, I do not know
what I should lament for the more, whether those
who were slain, or those whom they captured; or
those whom the devil has grievously ensnared with
the everlasting pain of Gehenna (hell-fire)—for they
will be chained together with him. 'For' indeed
'he who commits sin is a slave,'* [6] and is termed 'a
son of the devil.' †

3. Wherefore, let every man fearing God know
that they (the soldiers) are aliens from me, and from
Christ my God, for whom I discharge an embassage,
—patricides, fratricides, 'ravening wolves,' ‡ devour-
ing the people of the Lord as the food of bread. § [7]
As he says the ungodly 'have dissipated Thy law,
Lord.' ‖ [8] Since in these last times Ireland has
been most excellently and auspiciously planted and

* John viii. 34.　　† John viii. 44.　　‡ Acts xx. 29.
§ Psa. xiv. 4　　　　　　　　　　　　‖ Psa. cxix. 126.

instructed by the favour of God. I do not usurp
[other men's labours but] [9] I have part with those
whom He hath called and predestined to preach the
Gospel amidst no small persecutions, even to the
end of the earth; although the Enemy envies us by
the tyranny of Coroticus, who fears not God, nor
His priests, whom He hath chosen, and committed
to them that greatest, Divine, sublime power:
'Whom they bind upon earth, they are bound also
in heaven.' [10]

4. I, therefore, earnestly beseech (you), who are
holy and humble in heart, not to flatter such persons, nor to take food or drink with them, nor to
deem it right to take their alms — until they
rigorously do repentance with tears poured forth,
and make satisfaction to God, and liberate the servants of God, and the baptized handmaidens of
Christ, for whom He was put to death and crucified.

'The Most High reprobates the gifts of the
wicked. . . . He that offereth sacrifice of the goods
of the poor is as one that sacrificeth the son in the
presence of his father.' * [11] 'The riches,' he says,
'which he will collect unjustly shall be vomited
from his belly, the angel of death shall drag him off,
the fury of dragons shall assail him, the tongue of
the adder shall slay him, † [12] 'the inextinguishable
fire shall devour him.' ‡ And, therefore, 'Woe unto
those who fill themselves with things which are not
their own.' [13] Or, 'What doth it profit a man if
he gain the whole world, and suffer the loss of his
own soul ?' §

It were long to discuss (texts) one by one, or to
run through the whole law, to select testimonies
concerning such cupidity. Avarice is a deadly sin:

* Ecclus. xxxiv. 23, 24.   † Job xx. 15, 16.
‡ Matt. iii. 12.   § Matt. xvi. 26.

'Thou shalt not covet thy neighbour's goods.'[14]
'Thou shalt not kill.'* A murderer cannot be with
Christ. 'Whosoever hateth his brother is' termed
'a murderer.'† Or, 'He who loveth not his brother
abideth in death.'‡ [15] How much more guilty is
he who has stained his hands with the blood of the
sons of God—whom He lately acquired in the
ends of the earth by the exhortation of our littleness !' § [16]

5. Was it indeed without God, or according to
the flesh, that I came to Ireland?[17] Who compelled
me? I was bound by the Spirit not to see (again)
any of my kindred. Do I not love[18] pious compassion, because I act (thus) towards that nation which
once took me captive, and laid waste the servants
and handmaidens of my father's house? I was a
free-man according to the flesh, I was born of a
father who was a Decurio.[19] For I bartered my
noble-birth—I do not blush or regret it—for the
benefit of others. In fine, I am a servant in Christ,
(given over) to a foreign nation, on account of the
ineffable glory of that perennial life which is in
Christ Jesus our Lord. And if my own friends do
not acknowledge me :—'A prophet hath no honour
in his own country.'||

Perhaps (they think) we are not of the one sheep-
fold, nor have the one God as Father. As He
says : 'He that is not with Me is against Me ; and
he that gathereth not with Me scattereth.'¶ It is
not fitting that 'one destroys, another builds.' [20] I
do not seek those things which are my own. **[21]

6. Not my grace, but God, indeed, hath put this
desire into my heart, that I should be one of the

---

* Exod. xx. 13.   † 1 John iii. 15.   ‡ 1 John iii. 14.
§ Comp. 2 Cor. i. 15–17. || John iv. 44.
¶ Matt. xii. 30.   ** 2 Cor. xii. 14.

hunters or fishers, whom of old God promised before
in the last days.* [22]   I am envied. What shall I do,
Lord ?   I am greatly despised.   Behold ! Thy
sheep are torn around me, and are plundered even
by the above-mentioned robbers, by the order of
Coroticus, with hostile mind. Far from the love
of God is the betrayer of the Christians into the
hands of Scots and Picts !   Ravening wolves have
swallowed up the flock of the Lord,† which everywhere in Ireland was increasing with the greatest
diligence ; and the sons of the Scots and the
daughters of princes are monks and virgins of
Christ (in numbers) I cannot enumerate. Wherefore the injury done to the righteous will not give
thee pleasure (here), nor will it ever give pleasure in
the regions below.[23]

7. Which of the saints would not dread to be
sportive, or to enjoy a feast with such persons ?
They have filled their houses with the spoil of the
Christian dead. They live by rapine, they know
not (how) to pity. Poison (they drink), deadly food
they hand to their friends and sons. As Eve did not
understand that she offered death to her husband, so
are all those who do evil—they work out everlasting
death and perpetual punishment.

It is the custom of the Roman and Gallic Christians
to send holy and suitable men to the Franks,[24] and
to the other nations,[25] with so many thousands of
solidi,[26] to redeem baptized captives.[27] You (Coroticus) so often slay them—and sell them to a foreign
nation that knows not God ! You surrender members of Christ as into a den of wolves ! What hope
have you in God ? Or he, who either agrees with
you, or who uses to you words of flattery ?

8. God will judge.[28] For it is written, ' Not only

* Jer. xvi. 16.   † Comp. Acts xx. 29.

they who do evil, but also, they who consent thereto,
are to be condemned.' * 29   I know not what I can
say, or what I can speak further, concerning the
departed sons of God, whom the sword has touched
beyond measure severely.   For it is written, 'Weep
with them that weep,' † and again, 'If one member
suffers, all the members suffer along with it.' ‡ 30
Wherefore, the Church laments and bewails her
sons and daughters, whom the sword has not yet
slain, but who have been carried to distant parts,
and exported into far-off lands, where sin manifestly
is shamelessly stronger, [there it impudently dwells
and] abounds.   There free-born Christian men
having been sold are reduced to bondage—(bondage), too, of the most worthless, the vilest, and
apostate Piƈts !

9. Therefore, with sadness and sorrow I will
cry out, O my most beautiful and most beloved
brethren, and sons whom I begot in Christ—I cannot
count you—what shall I do for you ?   I am not
worthy, before God or men, to help !   The wicked-
ness of the wicked has prevailed against us.§ 31   We
are become as strangers.‖ 32   Perhaps they do not
believe that we have partaken of one baptism, or
that we have one God as Father.¶   To them it is a
disgrace that we have been born in Ireland ; 33 as he
says : 'Have ye not one God, why have ye forsaken
each his neighbour ?' ** 34   Therefore I grieve for
you, I do grieve, my most beloved ones.   But again,
I rejoice within myself, I have not laboured in vain,
and my pilgrimage has not been in vain ; 35—although
a crime so horrid and unspeakable has happened.
Thanks be to God, baptized believers, ye have passed

* Rom. i. 23.   † Rom. xii. 15.   ‡ 1 Cor. xii. 26.
§ Comp. Psa. lxv. 3.   ‖ Psa. lxix. 8.
¶ Comp. Eph. iv. 5.   ** Mal. ii. 10.

from this world to Paradise ! I see you have begun
to migrate 'where there shall be no night nor
grief, nor death any more,' * 36 but 'ye shall exult
as calves let loose from their bonds, and ye shall
tread down the wicked, and they shall be ashes
under your feet.' 37

10. Ye, therefore, shall reign with the apostles, and
prophets, and martyrs, and obtain the eternal kingdom,
as He Himself testifies, saying, ' They shall come from
the east and the west, and shall sit down with Abraham,
and Isaac, and Jacob, in the kingdom of heaven.' †
'Without are dogs, and sorcerers, and murderers,
and liars, and perjurers.' ‡ 38 'Their part is in the
lake of eternal fire.' § 39 Not without reason does
the Apostle say : 'Where the just will scarcely be
saved, where shall the sinner, and the impious, and the
transgressor of the law find himself ? ' ‖ 40 For where
will Coroticus with his most wicked rebels against
Christ, where shall they see themselves ? When
baptized women are distributed as rewards 41 on
account of a wretched temporal kingdom, which
indeed in a moment shall pass away like clouds or
smoke, which is dispersed everywhere by the wind !
So sinners and the fraudulent shall perish from the
face of the Lord, but the just shall feast with great
confidence with Christ ; they shall judge the nations,
and shall rule over wicked kings for ever and ever.
Amen.

11. I testify before God and His angels that it
shall be so, as He has intimated to my ignorance.
They are not my words, but those of God and of the
Apostles and Prophets, which I have set forth in
Latin,42—for they have never lied. 'He that
believeth . . . shall be saved ; but he that be-

* Rev. xxi. 4, 25. † Matt. viii. 11. ‡ Rev. xxii. 15.
§ Rev. xxi. 8. ‖ 1 Peter iv. 18,

lieveth not shall be condemned.'* 'God hath spoken.' † 43

I entreat earnestly, whosoever is a servant of God, that he may be prompt to be the bearer of this letter; that it in no way be abstracted by any one, but far rather that it be read before all the people, and in the presence of Coroticus himself. To the end, that if God would inspire them, that they may at some time return to God, or even though late may repent of what they have done so impiously—murderers of brethren in the Lord—and may liberate the baptized captives, whom they have taken before, so that they may deserve to live unto God, and may be made whole here and in eternity. Peace be to the Father, and the Son, and the Holy Ghost. Amen.

* Mark xvi. 16. † Psa. lx. 6.

The Doubtful Remains of Patrick.

❦

I.—SAYINGS OF PATRICK.

THE following *Dicta Patricii*, or Sayings of St. Patrick, are given in Latin in the Rolls edition of the *Tripartite Life*, p. 301, as contained at the end of the Notes by Muirchu Maccu-Machtheni in the Book of Armagh, fol. 9, a. i. They are, as Dr. Whitley Stokes observes, disconnected from the context in that MS., with the simple heading *Dicta Patricii*, and are in very rustic Latin. The character of their Latinity renders it highly probable that they may be genuine remains of the saint, while the manner in which the Greek Κύριε ἐλέεισον (*Lord, have mercy on us*) is transliterated into Latin (in Sayings No. 4 and 5) is sufficient to show how slight an acquaintance Patrick had with the Greek language. The latter point confutes Nicholson's arguments (on pp. 84, 85, 168 of his work), in which he seeks to

6

prove that 'St. Patrick read the Scriptures from the Greek language alone.'

We have for convenience sake numbered the Sayings, and append them here, with the addition of a few notes :—

1. 'I had the fear of God as the guide of my journey through the Gauls [*per Gallias*] and Italy, even in the islands which are in the Tyrrhenian Sea.'

> The latter portion of this saying, from 'through the Gauls,' is incorporated into Tírechán's notes or collections of facts concerning Patrick found in the Book of Armagh. (Rolls edition, p. 302.) Dr. W. Stokes says that these notes are said to have been 'written from the dictation or copied from a book (*ex ore vel libro*) of his foster-father or tutor, Bishop Altán of Ardbraccan, who died A.D. 656.' (Rolls edition of *Tripartite Life*, p. xci.) If the 'saying' be genuine, Patrick must have visited Italy. But the evidence is weak, and will not bear much weight to be put upon it.

2. 'From the world ye have passed on to Paradise.'

> The saying quoted occurs in the *Epistle to Coroticus*, § 9, p. 78.

3. 'Thanks be to God !'

> This saying, which is found in the *Coroticus*, p. 78, and in the *Confession*, pp. 54, 57, 64 (compare also pp. 60, 66, 68), is entitled, from the frequency of its occurrence, to be numbered separately. The saying is well

illustrated by the following story, given by
Muirchu in his Notes on St. Patrick's Life
(which are of the seventh century). Dáire,
the Irish chieftain, who afterwards gave the
site for a church at Armagh, sent to the saint
as a present a caldron of brass which had
been imported from across the sea. Patrick,
on receiving the gift, said simply, *Grazacham*
(*gratias agamus*, 'Let us give thanks,' *i.e.*, to
God). Dáire went back to his home, mutter-
ing, 'The man is a fool who said nothing but
grazacham for a brazen caldron of such a
size!' He then ordered his servants to go
and bring him back the caldron. They
went forthwith to the saint, and said, 'We
are going to take away the caldron.' Patrick
said again, '*Grazacham*, take it away.' They
accordingly took it back. When they returned, Dáire asked them, 'What did the
Christian say when you took it away?'
They answered that he said, '*Grazacham*.'
Dáire exclaimed, '*Grazacham*, when it was
given! *grazacham*, when it was taken away!
his saying is so good with those *grazachams*,
that his caldron shall be brought back to him
again!' (Rolls *Tripartite*, p. 291.) The
same story is repeated in the *Tripartite Life*
(which was written in the eleventh century)
at pp. 230, 231 of the Rolls edition. See
also Miss Cusack's *Life of St. Patrick*, p. 351,
Dr. Todd's *Life*, p. 471. On the story,
compare the words in Job i. 21 : 'The Lord
gave, and the Lord hath taken away; blessed
be the name of the Lord.'

4. 'The Church of the Scots, nay even of the

Romans, (chant) as Christians, so, that ye may be Romans, (chant) as it ought to be chanted with you, at every hour of prayer that praiseworthy sentence, *Curie lession, Christe lession* [" Lord, have mercy upon us," " Christ have mercy upon us."].'

> The Latin is : ' Aeclessia Scotorum, immo Romanorum, ut Christiani, ita ut Romani sitis, ut decantetur uobiscum oportet omni hora orationis uox illa laudabilis " Curie lessión, Christe lession." ' It is evidently corrupt with its three " ut "s. Dr. Whitley Stokes has suggested to me that it should be read thus : ' Aeclessia Scottorum immo Romanorum, ut Christiani ita et Romani sitis, et decantetur vobiscum ut oportet omni hora orationis vox illa laudabilis,' &c. It should then be translated :—

' Church of the Scots, nay of the Romans, as ye are Christians so also be Romans ; and let that praiseworthy sentence be chanted by you at every (canonical) hour, as it ought to be, " Lord, have mercy upon us, Christ, have mercy upon us." '

> It must not be forgotten that in the *Epistle to Coroticus* Patrick speaks of himself as a Roman and a freeman (see *Coroticus*, p. 76). He also there alludes to ' the Roman and Gallic Christians ' as superior to other Christians in civilisation. It is most natural, therefore, to interpret the meaning of this saying to be : Imitate the customs of those Christians whose higher civilisation is a matter of general acknowledgment, and follow their example by making use of the versicle in question.

5. 'Let every Church that follows me chant,
"Curie lession, Christe lession." Thanks be to
God!'

The words quoted by St. Patrick in these two
'sayings' are Κύριε ἐλέεισον, Χρίστε ἐλ εισον.

II.—PROVERBS OF PATRICK.

THE following twelve sayings, styled *Proverbia St. Patricii*, are given by Villanueva (see Introduction, p. 12), as, according to Jocelin, having been translated into Latin from the Irish. All these 'sayings,' with others, are also given in Latin in the 'Extracts from the Irish Canons' in the Rolls *Tripartite*, p. 507 ff. Their authenticity is, however, somewhat questionable, although the Biblical quotations are curiously similar to those found in the genuine writings.

1. 'Patrick says : " It is better for us to admonish the negligent, that crimes may not abound, than to blame the things that have been done." Solomon says : " It is better to reprove than to be angry."'

> The passage referred to is, however, not found in the Solomonic writings, but occurs in Ecclesiasticus (the Book of Jesus the Son of Sirach) xx. 1. The Latin, *melius est arguere quam irasci*, is different from the Vulg. and the Itala, *quam bonum est arguere quam irasci*.

2. 'Patrick says : "Judges of the Church ought not to have the fear of man, but the fear of God, because the fear of God is the beginning of wisdom" (Prov. i. 7).'

3. 'Judges of the Church ought not to have the wisdom of this world, "for the wisdom of this world is foolishness with God," but to have the "wisdom of God" (1 Cor. iii. 19 ; i. 21).'

4. 'Judges of the Church ought not to take gifts, because "gifts blind the eyes of the wise, and change the words of the just." '

> The passage referred to is Ecclesiasticus xx. 31, but the quotation is not exact. The words quoted by Patrick are, *munera excæcant oculos sapientium et mutant verba justorum*. The Itala and Vulgate have : *Xenia et dona excæcant oculos judicum, et quasi mutus in ore avertit correptiones eorum, i.e.,* 'Presents and gifts blind the eyes of judges, and make them dumb in the mouth, so that they cannot correct.' (*Douay Version.*) The rendering of the latter clause in the Douay Version is a paraphrase of the Latin and Greek.

5. 'Judges of the Church ought not to respect a person in judgment, "for there is no respect of persons with God " (Rom. ii. 11).'

6. 'Judges of the Church ought not to have worldly wisdom (*cautelam sæcularem*), but Divine examples (before them), for it does not become the servant of God to be crafty or cunning (*cautum aut astutum*).'

Villanueva explains *cautela sæcularis* as equivalent to the *sapientia carnis*, 'the wisdom of
the flesh,' or 'carnal wisdom,' of Rom. viii. 7.
Compare 1 Cor. iii. 19.

7. 'Judges of the Church ought not to be so
swift in judgment until they know how too true it
may be which is written, "Do not desire quickly
to be a judge."'

The passage cited is Eccles. vii. 6.　The
quotation is slightly different from the Vulg.
Patrick quotes the words, *noli judex esse cito*.
The Itala and Vulg. have, *noli quærere fieri
iudex*, 'Seek not to be made a judge.' (*Douay
Version.*)

8. 'Judges of the Church ought not to be voluble.'

The doctrine of St. Patrick here is akin to that
in James i. 19, 20.

9. 'Judges of the Church ought not to tell a lie,
for a lie is a great crime.'

Compare John viii. 44; Eph. iv. 25; Rev.
xxii. 15.

10. 'Judges of the Church ought to "judge just
judgment," "for with whatever judgment they shall
judge, it shall be judged to them."'

The first passage quoted is from John vii. 24.
The second passage is from Matt. vii. 2.
Patrick quotes the latter: *in quocunque judicio
judicaverint, judicabitur de illis*.　The Vulgate
is, *in quo enim judicio judicaveritis, judicabimini*,
'for with what judgment you judge, you
shall be judged.'　Similarly the Itala.

11. 'Patrick says : "Look into the examples of the elders, where you will find no guile." '

The Latin is : *exempla majorum perquire ubi nihil fallaciæ invenies.* By 'the elders' Villanueva considers Patrick means the saints, apostles, evangelists, and disciples of the Lord, and the fathers and doctors of the Church.

12. 'Patrick says : "Judges who do not judge rightly the judgments of the Church are not judges, but falsifiers (*falsatores*)." '

III.—THE STORY OF PATRICK AND THE ROYAL DAUGHTERS.

THE following story, which is given in Tirechan's collection, found in the Book of Armagh, bears internal evidence of its antiquity and genuineness. 'The naïveté of the questions asked by the girls about God and His sons and daughters' is one of these striking evidences, for they are, as Whitley Stokes observes, 'questions which no mere legendmonger ever had the imagination to invent.' The narrative is quite superior to the surroundings in which it occurs in Tírechán (Rolls *Tripartite*, p. 314), or in the later *Tripartite Life* (pp. 99 ff.). We have translated it from the former, adding in the notes the more important readings found in the *Tripartite Life*.

But thence went the holy Patrick to the spring which is called Clebach,* on the sides of Crochan,† towards the rising of the sun, before the rising of

---

* Cliabach. (*Trip.*)   † Cruachan. (*Trip.*)

the sun, and they sat beside the springs.   And
behold two daughters of Loegaire,* Éthne the fair,
and Fedelm the ruddy, came to the spring in the
morning, after the custom of women, to wash,† and
they found a holy synod of bishops with Patrick by
the spring.‡   And they did not know from whence
they were, or of what shape, or of what people, or
of what region.   But they thought that they were
men of the *side*, or of the terrestrial gods, or an
apparition.§   And the daughters said to them—
    'Whence are ye, and whence have ye come?'
    And Patrick said to them—
    'It were better that you would confess our true
God than to inquire about our race.'
    The first daughter said, 'Who is God?   And
where is God?   And of what is God?   And where
is His dwelling-place?   Has your God sons and
daughters, gold and silver?   Is He ever-living?   Is
He beautiful?   Have many fostered His Son?   Are
His daughters dear and beautiful to the men of the
world?   Is He in heaven or on earth?   In the sea?
in the rivers? in the mountains? in the valleys?
Tell us how is He seen?   How is He loved?
How is He found?   Is He in youth? or in
age?'‖
    But holy Patrick, full of the Holy Spirit, answer-
ing, said—

* 'Loegaire, son of Niall.'   (*Trip.*)
† 'to wash their hands.'   (*Trip.*)
‡ 'the maidens found beside the well the assembly of clerics
in white garments, with their books before them.'   (*Trip.*)
§ 'And they wondered at the shape of the clerics, and thought
that they were men of the elves or apparitions.'   (*Trip.*)   Dr.
Whitley Stokes' note on Tírechán is, '*Firu síde*, "males of the
síde" or terrestrial gods, corresponding, perhaps, with the θεοὶ
χθόνιοι or Inferi.'
‖ The questions are somewhat transposed in the *Tripartite
Life*, but are substantially identical.

'Our God is the God of all men, the God of heaven and earth, of the sea, and of the rivers; the God of the sun and of the moon, of all the stars; the God of the lofty mountains and of the lowly valleys; the God over heaven and in heaven and under heaven. He has His dwelling towards heaven and earth, and the sea, and all things which are in them. He inspires all things, He gives life to all things, He surpasses all things, He supports all things. He kindles the light of the sun, He strengthens the light of the moon at night for watches;* and He made springs in the arid land, and dry islands in the sea; and the stars He placed to minister to the greater lights. He has a Son co-eternal with Himself and like unto Himself. The Son is not younger than the Father, nor is the Father older than the Son. The Father, Son, and Holy Spirit are not separated. I truly desire to unite you to the Heavenly King, since ye are daughters of an earthly king. Believe (on Him).'

And the daughters said, as if with one mouth and heart—

'How can we believe on the Heavenly King? Teach us most diligently, so that we may see Him face to face. Point out to us, and we will do whatsoever thou shalt say to us.'

And Patrick said: 'Do you believe that the sin of your father and mother is taken away by baptism?'

They replied: 'We do believe it.'

[*Patrick*] 'Do you believe that there is repentance after sin?'

[*Daughters*] 'We do believe it.'

[*Patrick*] 'Do you believe that there is a life after

* This is a conjectural translation. The Latin is [*lunæ*] *lumen noctis ad* [MS. *et*] *notitias valat.*

death ? Do you believe in the resurrection in the day of judgment ? '

[*Daughters*] ' We do believe it.'

[*Patrick*] 'Do you believe in the unity of the Church ? '

[*The Daughters*] ' We do believe it.'

And they were baptized, and [Patrick placed] a white garment * on their heads.

And they begged to see the face of Christ.

And the saint said to them : ' Unless you shall have tasted death, you cannot see the face of Christ, and unless you shall receive the sacrifice.' †

And they replied : ' Give to us the sacrifice, that we may see the Son our spouse.'

And they received the Eucharist of God, and they slept in death. And they placed them in a bed covered with one mantle, and their friends made a wailing and a great lamentation. . . . And the days of the wailing for the daughters of the king were ended, and they buried them by the spring *Clebach*, and they made a round ditch in the likeness of a *ferta* [*a grave*], because so the Scotic men and Gentiles used to do. But, with us it is called *relic*, that is, the *remains* and *feurt*.

The latter few lines of the story are slightly different in the *Tripartite Life*. It will be observed that the doctrine set forth with regard to the two sacraments is somewhat questionable. But it must

---

* The white garment of baptism worn for eight days by the newly-baptized in the ancient church. See *Coroticus*, p. 68. Some Roman Catholic writers have endeavoured to explain this that the virgins took the veil, but that is not the meaning. See Dr. Todd's *St. Patrick*, p. 456.

† Instead of ' the sacrifice,' the *Tripartite Life* has, ' unless ye receive Christ's body and His blood.'

be remembered that errors on those points were prevalent in the Church of the fifth century. The story in general is one of considerable beauty, and is worthy to be preserved as a genuine fragment of a striking missionary incident in the early part of that century.

IV.—PATRICK'S VISION OF THE FUTURE OF IRELAND.

THE following account of our saint's vision concerning the future of Ireland is given in Jocelin's *Life of St. Patrick*, in chapter clxxv. As it is referred to in Rev. Robert King's valuable *Primer of the History of the Irish Church* (3 vols., Dublin, 1845–51), we give it in full here, with Jocelin's exposition.

And the man of God was anxiously desiring, and earnestly praying, that he might be certified of the present and future state of Hibernia, to the end that he might know with what devotion of faith he was burning, and also the value of his labour in the sight of God. Then the Lord heard the desire of his heart and manifested that which he sought for unto him by an evident revelation.

For while he was engaged in prayer, and the heart of his mind was opened, he beheld the whole island to be as it were a flaming fire ascending unto heaven, and he heard the Angel of God saying unto

him, 'Such at this time is Hibernia in the sight of
the Lord.' And after a little space he beheld in
all parts of the island cone-like mountains of fire
stretching unto the skies. And again, after a little
space, he beheld as it were candlesticks burning,
and after a while darkness intervened ; and then he
beheld scanty lights, and at length he beheld coals
lying hidden here and there, as reduced unto ashes,
yet appearing still burning.

And the Angel added : 'What thou seest here
shown in different states are the Irish nations.'
Then the saint, weeping exceedingly, repeated
often the words of the Psalmist, saying : 'Will
God cast off for ever, and will He be no more
entreated ? Shall His mercy come to an end from
generation to generation ? Shall God forget to be
merciful, and shut up His mercy in His displeasure ?'

And the Angel said, 'Look towards the northern
side, and on the right hand of an height shalt thou
behold the darkness dispersed from the face of the
light which thenceforth will arise.'

Then the saint raised his eyes, and behold, he at
first saw a small light arising in Ulidia, the which
struggled a long time with the darkness, and at
length dispersed it, and illumined with its rays the
whole island. Nor ceased the light to increase and
to prevail, even until it had restored to its former
fiery state all Hibernia.

Then was the heart of St. Patrick filled with joy,
and his tongue with exultation, giving thanks for
all these things which had been shown unto him
by grace. And he understood in the greatness of
this fiery ardour of the Christian faith, the devotion
and zeal for religion wherewith those islanders
burned. By the fiery mountains he understood the

saints, illustrious by miracles and words and by their
examples. By the diminution of the light, the de-
crease of holiness. By the darkness that covered
the land, the infidelity prevailing therein. By the
intervals of delay, the distances of the succeeding
times.

But the people think the period of darkness was
that in which Gurmundus and Turgesius, heathen
Norwegian princes, conquered and ruled in Hibernia. For in those days the saints, like coals
covered with ashes, lay hidden in caves and dens
from the face of the wicked, who pursued them all
the day like sheep for the slaughter. Whence it
happened that differing rites and new sacraments,
which were contrary to the ecclesiastical institutions,
were introduced into the Church and by prelates
of the Holy Church ignorant of the Divine law.
But the light arising first from the northern part, and
after long conflict exterminating the darkness, those
born in Hibernia assert to be St. Malachy, who pre-
sided first in the Church at Dunum [Down], after-
ward in the metropolis, Ardmachia [Armagh], and
reduced the island unto the Christian law. On the
other hand, the people of Britain ascribe this light
to their coming, for that then the Church seemed
under their rule to be advanced unto a better state ;
and that then religion seemed to be planted and
propagated, and the sacraments of the Church, and
the institutions of the Christian law, to be observed
with more regular observance.

But I do not pretend to decide of this contention,
neither do I solve it, but I think that the discussion and the decision thereof should be left to the
Divine Judgment.

Jocelin's *Life of St. Patrick* is given in *Messing-*

*hami Florilegium Insulæ Sanctorum seu Vitæ et Acta
Sanctorum Hiberniæ*, &c., Parisiis, 1624. A translation of this work into English, rather free in many
places, but sufficiently close to give a good idea of
the original, appeared in 1809—namely, *The Life
and Acts of St. Patrick, the Archbishop, Primate, and
Apostle of Ireland*, now first translated from the
original Latin of Jocelin, the Cistercian Monk of
Furnes, who flourished in the early part of the
twelfth century; with the elucidations of David
Rothe, Bishop of Ossory. By EDMUND L. SWIFT,
Esq. Dublin : Printed for the Hibernian Press Com-
pany by James Blyth, 1809. Our translation is taken
from the original. Much interesting matter is contained in *Messingham's Florilegium*, but the account of
this vision in Jocelin's *Life* appears to us one of the
few grains of wheat in a bushel of rubbish. Jocelin
had, however, access to works now lost, and hence
there may be something genuine in this vision. It
is at any rate interesting. King gives in his *History*
an attempt at a Protestant interpretation of this
prophecy. It is certainly susceptible of being
explained of the light of the Reformation ; and
was most suitably applied to the light diffused
throughout Ireland by means of Trinity College,
Dublin, in the congratulatory address presented to
that university on its tercentenary in 1892 by the
Prorector and Senatus of the University of Heidel-
berg.

V.—A NEWLY-DISCOVERED CONFES-SION ATTRIBUTED TO ST. PATRICK.

INTRODUCTORY REMARKS.

FRESH contribution to the Patrician literature has recently appeared in the *Revue Celtique* (Vol. xv., No. 2) for April, 1894. Paris: Librairie Emile Bouillon, editor: published under the superintendence of eminent Celtic scholars. The chief editors are H. d'Arbois de Jubainville, Membre de l'Institut, Professor in the College de France, with J. Loth, Dean of the Faculty of Letters at Rennes ; E. Ernault, Professor of the Faculty of Letters at Poitiers, and G. Dottin, Master of Conferences of the Faculty of Letters at Rennes, Editorial Secretary. The article is written by M. Samuel Berger, Professor in the Protestant Theological Faculty, Paris, and is entitled, *Confession des Péchés attribuée a saint Patrice.*

This Confession is given by M. Berger in the original Latin, of which we subjoin a translation in English, in order to render our edition of *The Writings of St. Patrick* as complete as possible.

M. Berger states in the opening note to his article

that this confession was discovered in the library of
the town of Angers, capital of the Department of
Maine and Loire. The manuscript is numbered
Angers 14, and is a MS. of the ninth, or rather of the
ninth or tenth century. The Confessio begins at
folio 180 verso, at the end of the Gallican Psalter,
immediately followed by canticles and a litany, in
which are invocations addressed to the saints of
the centre and north of France (from Bourges and
Poitiers to Cologne and Liege), together with St.
Boniface, St. Columba, and St. Gall. St. Boniface
was an English missionary; but St. Columba and St.
Gall, it may be noted, were both missionaries from
Ireland. The Confession of St. Patrick is followed
at folio 183 verso by the 'Confessio quam beatus
Alcuinus composuit Domino Karolo imperatori,' or
the confession which St. Alcuin composed for the
use of the Emperor Charles the Great. Alcuin was
a native of York, trained and educated in that city.
He established a school in connection with the monastery of Tours about A.D. 796. The MS. contains
other pieces, especially prayers. M. Berger thinks
the MS. must have been written at Tours, for the
writing exhibits the marks specially characteristic
of the MSS. written in that famous monastery.
Tours, it must be remembered, is not very far distant
further up the Loire.

When one examines into the style of the
Confessio before us, it cannot be denied that its
Latin is very different from that which appears in
the Confession or autobiography preserved in the
Book of Armagh and the other ancient MSS.
noticed in our Introduction. In a piece of this
character, copied into the Angers MS., as a
confession for the use of private Christians, and
not because of any special value in relation to the

life of St. Patrick himself, the scribe might have had no scruple whatever in correcting, according to his ability, instances of faulty Latin, such as abound in St. Patrick's own writings. It would also be natural to make St. Patrick's quotations from Scripture conform to the Vulgate version which was in common use for ages prior to the ninth century. Although there are cases of doubtful Latinity in the Latin original edited by M. Berger, it is clear that St. Patrick could not have written Latin as pure as that found in this MS. The Latinity of the piece may not, for the reason stated, be quite conclusive against its Patrician authorship. Nor is the Patrician authorship conclusively disproved by the fact that the Bible quotations, where not loosely quoted from memory, are in this confession all derived from the Vulgate.

M. Berger observes that these books of penitence appear to have come originally from Ireland. Books of that kind seem to have been designed to teach those who used them how to make their humble confessions before God in prayer. M. Berger remarks that the names of authors are in several cases apparently assigned to them at random. He remarks that the *Penitential* of St. Columba is the first work in the series of such compositions, the authenticity of which can be affirmed with certainty. He considers the Confession of Angers to be probably a genuine Irish work, although it is more than doubtful that St. Patrick was its author. But when we reflect on the close connection into which the monastery of Tours, where it was probably written, was brought with Ireland, it is possible that the scribe may have had evidence in favour of the Patrician authorship, which has not come down to us. In its present form the language of this Confessio, if a work of St. Patrick, must have undergone considerable revision, a revision which, under the circumstances, was natural and justifiable.

Turning next to internal evidence, if the piece be regarded as a personal confession of sins, and not one drawn up for the use of converts, there are several points which are inconsistent with St. Patrick's genuine writings. Though he was fully aware from our Lord's teaching in the Sermon on the Mount that sins of uncleanness may be committed by evil thoughts as well as by evil actions, it is difficult to suppose that St. Patrick could have been guilty of such transgressions as this Confession would lead us to conclude. He denies explicitly in his genuine Confession (see pp. 68, 69) that he ever received gifts, while in this newly-found Confession he confesses himself guilty of that sin.

Whatever St. Patrick's early career may have been, and, according to his own statements, prior to his captivity he did not live a holy life (see pp. 47, 50, 58, 61), it is hard to imagine he could have had opportunity to transgress in the way of gluttony and riotous living as described in this writing.

After careful consideration of the composition, we must therefore view it, not as designed to be a record of the author's own personal frailties, but rather as a touchstone by which his converts might examine into their individual lives.

Two points, however, in this newly-discovered Confession are in favour of its belonging to the age of St. Patrick—namely, the reference to sinning by divinations (compare stanza 6 of the Irish hymn), and to sinning by partaking of polluted food. The story of St. Patrick's being tempted to eat honey offered in sacrifice to idols, as told in the genuine Confession at p. 54, may illustrate the latter.

The last ten lines of the special confession of sins do appear to have a sort of Patrician ring about them.

The doctrine of the Angers Confession is in harmony with the primitive faith set forth in St. Patrick's writings. There is not one word in it which contains the slightest allusion to the invocation of saints or angels, although angels are alluded to as witnesses of the sins of men. Christ is described as being alone without sin, a doctrine inconsistent with the late mediæval notion of the sinlessness of the Virgin Mary.

It is important also to note that there is no reference in the Confession to any 'auricular confession' made to a priest; and the expressions used in the commencement of the last paragraph which speak of Christ as the High Priest to whom sin is to be confessed, are opposed to any such practice.

Although it is true that this confession of sins is 'drawn up without any order,' and that, short as it is, it contains various repetitions, the doctrine set forth is highly Evangelical. And as it is probably of an Irish type, it seems to prove that the doctrines of the Irish missionaries of that date were in the main pure and Scriptural. The Divinity of Christ —for the composition is a confession addressed to Christ, and to Him alone—is unmistakably affirmed. There are but two allusions to God the Father, and one to the Holy Spirit, which all occur at the end of the first paragraph.

This new discovery is then of sufficient importance to justify our exhibiting here a complete translation of its text.

[HERE] BEGINS THE CONFESSION OF SAINT PATRICK,
BISHOP.

God, my God, omnipotent King, I humbly adore
Thee. Thou art King of kings, Lord of lords.[1]
Thou art the Judge of every age.[2] Thou art the
Redeemer of souls. Thou art the Liberator of those
who believe. Thou art the Hope of those who toil.
Thou art the Comforter of those in sorrow. Thou
art the Way to those who wander. Thou art Master
to the nations.[3] Thou art the Creator of all creatures.
Thou art the Lover of all good. Thou art the Prince
of all virtues. Thou art the joy of all Thy saints.
Thou art life perpetual.[4] Thou art joy in truth.[5]
Thou art the exultation in the eternal fatherland.[6]
Thou art the Light of light.[7] Thou art the Fountain
of holiness. Thou art the glory of God the Father
in the height. Thou art Saviour of the world. Thou
art the plenitude of the Holy Spirit. Thou sittest
at the right hand of God the Father on the throne,
reigning for ever.

I seek for forgiveness of my sins, O my God, Jesus
Christ. Thou art He who desirest no one to perish,
' but will have all men saved, and to come to the
knowledge of the truth.'[8] Thou, O God, with Thy
holy and chaste mouth hast said : In whatever day
the sinner may be converted ' living he shall live and
shall not die.'[9] I will return to Thee, O God, and
with all my heart[10] will cry to Thee, my God, and
to Thee now I desire to confess my sins. My transgressions are multiplied above me,[11] because my sins
have no number before Thine eyes. O Lord, I
appear [*i.e.,* stand before Thee] a witness accused
by conscience. I dare not ask what I do not deserve
to obtain. For Thou knowest, Lord, all things which
are done in us, and we blush to confess what by

ourselves [12] we do not fear to commit. In words alone [tantum] we obey Thee, in heart we lie. And what we do not say we desire we approve of by our acts.[13] Spare, Lord, those confessing, pardon those sinning. Pity those asking Thee, for in Thy mysteries my perception is weak.[14] Show, Lord, Thou who dost not receive prayers [verba] from us [15] with hard heart, that through Thee Thou mayest bestow pardon on us, O Jesus Christ our Lord.[16]

I will confess to Thee, my God, because I have sinned in heaven and in earth,[17] and before Thee, and before Thy angels, and before the face of all Thy saints.

I have sinned by negligence of Thy commands and of my deeds.

I have sinned by pride and by envy.

I have sinned by detraction and by avarice.

I have sinned by luxury [18] and by malice.

I have sinned by fornication and by gluttony.[19]

I have sinned by false testimony and by hatred of men.

I have sinned by theft and by robbery [rapinam].

I have sinned by blasphemy and by the desire of the flesh.

I have sinned by drunkenness and by hateful tales.

I have sinned by contentions and by quarrelling.

I have sinned by swearing and anger.

I have sinned by earthly and transitory joy.

I have sinned by fear and by the weakness (?) of my mind [suavitatem mentis meæ].

I have sinned by deceit and by murmuring.

I have sinned by the instability of faith of mind, and by the impiety of doubt.[20]

I have sinned by unmercifulness and by despising of men.

I have sinned by corrupt and wicked works [&] judgments.

I have sinned by negligence and by forgetfulness of the works of God.

I have sinned by wandering and subtlety of my mind.[21]

I have sinned by impatience and by imperfection of hope.

I have sinned by hardness and by blindness of heart and mind.

I have sinned by forgetfulness [22] of the love of God and of my neighbour.

I have sinned by disobedience and by the loss of good ordinances.[23]

I have sinned by the loss of heavenly desires and by the love of earthly things.

I have sinned by inclinations to evil, and by deceitful arguments.

I have sinned by evil examples, and by the uncleanness of humanity.

I have sinned by vain melancholy,[24] and by stupor of mind.

I have sinned by feigned humility, and loss of the love of God.

I have sinned by cursing, and by divinations.[25]

I have sinned by the non-accomplishment of my vows and by wicked inventions.

I have sinned by [over-] investigation [26] of the majesty of God, and of heavenly life.

I have sinned by pomps of the body, and by canvassing for the favours of men.

I have sinned by the intemperance of mirth and madness.

I have sinned by laziness and indolence of mind.

I have sinned by counsels of iniquity, and by returning of evil.

I have sinned by concupiscence and by perpetration of lust.

I have sinned by consent to, and by knowledge of, evil acts and words.

I have sinned by works upon the Lord's day and by illuring imaginations.[27]

I have sinned by sorrow of the world,[28] and by love of money,[29] and by ambitions after honours.

I have sinned by restlessness and by bitterness of mind.

I have sinned by useless joy, and by scurrility, by grievous words, and by intemperance of clamour.

I have sinned by desperation, and by impurity of confession.

I have sinned by imperfection, and negligence of amendment.

I have sinned by presumption and despair.

I have sinned by acceptance of unjust gifts and by the punishments of impious acts.

I have sinned by pretence, and by pleasing of myself.

I have sinned by silence concerning righteousness, and iniquity, and flattery.

I have sinned by rioting [30] and by taking of polluted food, [31] and by suggestions of the devil, and by the delight of the spirit, and by knowledge of the flesh.

I have sinned in my eyes and in my ears.

I have sinned in my hands, and in my mouth, and in my lips, and in all my deeds.

I have sinned in tongue and in throat.

I have sinned in neck and in breast.

I have sinned in heart and in cogitations.

I have sinned in mind and in operations.

I have sinned in hands and in feet.

I have sinned in bones and in flesh.

I have sinned in marrow and in veins.

I have sinned in my mind and in my whole body.

If now Thy vengeance will be upon me as great as my sins have been multiplied in myself, how shall I sustain Thy judgment? But I have Thee as the High Priest [32] to whom I confess all my sins. [I do] that to Thee alone, my God, [33] because 'I have sinned against Thee alone, [34] and done evil before Thee.' [35] And because Thou art, O God, alone without sin, I beseech Thee, O Lord my God, by Thy passion, and by the sign of Thy salvation-bringing cross, and by the shedding of Thy blood, in order that Thou mayest grant to me remission of all my sins. I beg Thee, my Lord Jesus Christ, that Thou wilt not render to me according to my deserving, but according to Thy great compassion. Judge me, O Lord, according to the judgment of Thy indulgence. I beg Thee and I adjure Thee, O my God omnipotent, that Thou mayest plant in me Thy love and fear. Awake in me repentance of my sins, and sorrow, for Thy name's sake. Give to me the remembrance of Thy commands, and assist me, O my God, blot out my iniquity from Thy sight, and turn not away Thy face from my prayer. 'Cast me not out from Thy presence.' [36] Leave me not, my God, neither depart from me, but confirm me in Thy will. Teach me what I ought not to do, what to do, or to speak, what to keep silent. Defend me, O Lord my God, against the darts of the devil, and against the angel of hell suggesting and teaching many evil things. [37] Do not desert me, O Lord my God, nor leave Thy miserable servant, but assist me, my God, and perform in me Thy teaching. [38] Teach me to do Thy will, because Thou art my teacher and my God, [39] who reignest for ever and ever. Amen.

Appendix.

IT will no doubt be interesting to our readers to be presented here with some poetical translations of St. Patrick's Hymn. The first is that by James Clarence Mangan, a talented but unfortunate Irish poet. It originally appeared in *Duffy's Magazine*, and was afterwards reprinted in a volume of Mangan's collected *Poems, with a Biographical Introduction* by John Mitchell (New York, 1859). It was also given in the appendix to the first edition of *The College Irish Grammar*, by Rev. Ulick J. Bourke (Dublin, O'Daly, 1856), and later in Canon McIlwaine's *Lyra Hibernica*, Belfast, Dublin, and London, 2nd ed., 1879. The translation is a very spirited one, and 'preserves,' as Dr. Todd remarks in his work on *St. Patrick, the Apostle of Ireland*, 'the tone and spirit of the original.' It must be remembered that this version was founded on the translation originally made by Dr. Petrie, and therefore has the error of translating the opening words of the hymn 'At Tara,' as well as others mentioned in our notes. (See note 2, p. 121.)

I.

St. Patrick's Hymn before Tara.

I.

At Tara to-day, in this awful hour,
  I call on the Holy Trinity !
Glory to Him who reigneth in power,
The God of the elements, Father and Son,
And paraclete Spirit, which Three are the One
  The everlasting Divinity !

II.

At Tara to-day, I call on the Lord,
On Christ, the Omnipotent Word,
Who came to redeem from death and sin,
    Our fallen race ;
    And I put, and I place,
  The virtue that lieth in
  His incarnation lowly,
  His baptism pure and holy,
His life of toil, and tears, and affliction,
His dolorous death, His crucifixion,
His burial, sacred, and sad, and lone,
His resurrection to life again,
His glorious ascension to heaven's high throne,
And lastly, His future dread
And terrible coming to judge all men—
Both the living and the dead.

III.

At Tara to-day, I put and I place,
  The virtue that dwells in the seraphim's love ;
And the virtue and grace
  That are in the obedience.

And unshaken allegiance,
Of all the archangels and angels above ;
And in the hope of the resurrection
To everlasting reward and election ;
And in the prayers of the fathers of old ;
And in the truths the prophets foretold ;
And in the apostles' manifold preaching ;
And in the confessors' faith and teaching ;
And in the purity ever-dwelling
  Within the Immaculate Virgin's * breast ;
And in the actions bright and excelling,
  Of all good men, the just and the best.

iv.

At Tara to-day, in this fateful hour,
I place all heaven with its power,
And the sun with its brightness,
And the snow with its whiteness,
And fire with all the strength it hath,
And lightning with its rapid wrath,
And the winds with their swiftness along their
      path,
And the sea with its deepness,
And the rocks with their steepness,
And the earth with its starkness,
  All these I place,
  By God's almighty help and grace,
Between myself and the powers of darkness.

* The translator has here taken an unwarranted liberty with
the hymn, which does not contain any reference to the Virgin
Mary. The term 'immaculate' is, of course, highly objectionable, as introducing an epithet which would be interpreted by all
as referring to the novel dogma of 'the immaculate conception.'
The term 'immaculate' might in itself be defensible in the loose
sense of 'stainless,' *i.e.*, one whose life was pure and unspotted.

v.

At Tara to-day,
May God be my stay !
May the strength of God now nerve me !
May the power of God preserve me !
May God the Almighty be near me !
May God the Almighty espy me !
May God the Almighty hear me !
   May God give me eloquent speech !
May the arm of God protect me !
May the wisdom of God direct me !
May God give me power to teach and to
   preach !
May the shield of God defend me !
May the host of God attend me,
      And warn me,
      And guard me,
Against the wiles of demons and devils ;
Against temptations of vice and evils ;
Against the bad passions and wrathful will
   Of the reckless mind and the wicked heart ;
Against every man that designs me ill,
Whether leagued with others, or plotting apart.

vi.

In this hour of hours,
I place all those powers,
Between myself and every foe,
   Who threatens my body and soul
   With danger or dole ;
To protect me against the evils that flow
From lying soothsayers' incantations ;
From the gloomy laws of the Gentile nations ;
From heresy's hateful innovations ;
From idolatry's rites and invocations :

By these my defenders,
    My guards against every ban—
And spells of smiths, and Druids, and women ;
In fine, against every knowledge that renders
The light Heaven sends us, dim in
    The spirit and soul of man !

VII.

May Christ, I pray,
Protect me to-day,
Against poison and fire ;
Against drowning and wounding ;
That so in His grace abounding,
I may earn the preacher's hire !

VIII.

Christ as a light
Illumine and guide me !
Christ as a shield o'ershadow and cover me !
Christ be under me ! Christ be over me !
    Christ be beside me,
    On left hand and right !
Christ be before me, behind me, about me !
Christ, this day, be within and without me !

IX.

Christ the lowly and meek,
Christ the all-powerful, be
In the heart of each to whom I speak,
In the mouth of each who speaks to me,
    In all who draw near me,
    Or see me, or hear me !
    8

X.

At Tara to-day, in this awful hour,
　　I call on the Holy Trinity!
Glory to Him who reigneth in power,
The God of the elements, Father and Son,
And paraclete Spirit, which Three are the One,
　　The everlasting Divinity!

XI.

Salvation dwells with the Lord,
With Christ, the Omnipotent Word,
From generation to generation,
Grant us, O Lord, Thy grace and salvation!

II.

THE following version is from the facile pen of
the late Mrs. Alexander, wife of the present Archbishop of Armagh.　It is closer to the original than
the preceding, the latest corrections made by Dr.
Whitley Stokes being used.　It has been issued, pointed
and accentuated for chanting, by the Irish Christian
Knowledge Association.　Mrs. Alexander's version
is now widely used in Ireland, in the services of the
Church of Ireland on St. Patrick's Day, and on other
occasions.　It was sung at York Minster as a pro-
cessional hymn on St. Patrick's Day, 1891, when
Archbishop Magee, who was an Irishman, was en-
throned (see pp. 14, 15).　The version was appended
to this work by the kind permission of Mrs. Alexander.

I bind unto myself to-day
　　The strong name of the Trinity,
By invocation of the same,
　　The Three in One and One in Three.

I bind this day to me for ever,
   By power of faith, Christ's Incarnation ;
His baptism in Jordan river ;
   His death on cross for my salvation ;
His bursting from the spicèd tomb ;
   His riding up the heavenly way ;
His coming at the day of doom ;
   I bind unto myself to-day.

I bind unto myself the power
   Of the great love of Cherubim ;
The sweet 'Well done' in judgment hour ;
   The service of the Seraphim,
Confessors' faith, Apostles' word,
   The Patriarchs' prayers, the Prophets' scrolls,
All good deeds done unto the Lord,
   And purity of virgin souls.

I bind unto myself to-day
   The virtues of the star-lit heaven,
The glorious sun's life-giving ray,
   The whiteness of the moon at even,
The flashing of the lightning free,
   The whirling wind's tempestuous shocks,
The stable earth, the deep salt sea,
   Around the old eternal rocks.

I bind unto myself to-day
   The power of God to hold and lead,
His eye to watch, His might to stay,
   His ear to hearken to my need.
The wisdom of my God to teach,
   His hand to guide, His shield to ward ;
The Word of God to give me speech,
   His heavenly host to be my guard.

Against the demon snares of sin,
   The vice that gives temptation force,
The natural lusts that war within,
   The hostile men that mar my course ;
Or few or many, far or nigh,
   In every place, and in all hours,
Against their fierce hostility,
   I bind to me these holy powers.

Against all Satan's spells and wiles,
   Against false words of heresy,
Against the knowledge that defiles,
   Against the heart's idolatry,
Against the wizard's evil craft,
   Against the death-wound and the burning
The choking wave, the poisoned shaft,
   Protect me, Christ, till Thy returning.

Christ be with me, Christ within me,
   Christ behind me, Christ before me,
Christ beside me, Christ to win me,
   Christ to comfort and restore me,
Christ beneath me, Christ above me,
   Christ in quiet, Christ in danger,
Christ in hearts of all that love me,
   Christ in mouth of friend and stranger.

I bind unto myself the Name,
   The strong Name of the Trinity ;
By invocation of the same,
   The Three in One, and One in Three.
Of Whom all nature hath creation ;
   Eternal Father, Spirit, Word :
Praise to the Lord of my salvation,
   Salvation is of Christ the Lord.

III.

THE following metrical version appeared in the columns of the *Irish Ecclesiastical Gazette* for April 5, 1889. Its author, the late J. J. Murphy, Esq., was a well-known and valued writer, and for many years Hon. Sec. of the Diocesan Synod of the Diocese of Down, Connor, and Dromore. We quote Mr. Murphy's remarks :—

'In offering a new metrical version of this poem, I do not mean to challenge comparison with Mrs. Alexander's. Hers is meant to be sung as a hymn, for which purpose mine is not suitable.

'The irregular stanzas of this version represent those of the original. The Latin verses which conclude the Irish original are translated by longer lines than the rest.

'I have made this version partly from the translation in Stokes's and Wright's "Writings of St. Patrick," and partly from Dr. Todd's [see p. 15].

JOSEPH JOHN MURPHY.'

I bind as armour on my breast
    The Threefold Name whereon I call,
Of Father, Son, and Spirit blest,
    The Maker and the Judge of all.

I bind as armour on my breast
The power in flesh made manifest
Of Him, the Son, from Heaven who came,
    His baptism in the Jordan's wave,
His cross of pain and bitter shame,
    His burial, and His opened grave ;
And God's eternal power, whereby
He rose, ascended up on high,
    And will return to judge and save.

In hope a heavenly crown to win,
    I bind as armour on my breast
The obedience and the love wherein
    Angels and seraphs are possessed,
With faithful prayer and worthy deed
    Of all the saints in history's roll,
Who kept unstained their holy creed
    And virgin purity of soul.

As armour on my breast I bind
    The powers of God in heaven and earth ;
The fleetness of the rushing wind,
    The brightness of the morning's birth ;
The splendour of the fiery glow,
The whiteness of the winter snow,
    The lightning's wildly flashing mirth ;
The strength that girds the rocky steep,
The vastness of the unfathomed deep.

I bind as armour on my breast
    The Wisdom which shall be my guide ;
The Shield whose shelter bids me rest
    In peace, whatever ills betide ;
The Eye of God, to search my thought ;
    His Ear, my prayer of faith to hear ;
His Word, to make my words be fraught
    With courage which His foes shall fear ;
His angel host, to guard my path
Against all human guile and wrath,
Against the tempter's lures to sin,
Against the lusts that strive within.

All these upon my breast I bind
    Against my foes in earth and hell ;
    Against the sorcerer's chanted spell,
And sway of idols o'er the mind ;

Falsehoods of heresy, and powers
That rule the heathen in the hours
   Of darkness ; women's evil wiles ;
   And all the knowledge that defiles.

Guard me and shield me, Christ, my Lord !
   Guard me against my foe's desire ;
   Guard me in dangers of the fire,
   Guard me in dangers of the sea ;
   Guard me, O Lord, in serving Thee,
And make me share the great reward.

Christ be within me and around ;
   Christ on my left hand and my right ;
May Christ in all my thoughts be found,
   Christ in all breadth, and depth, and height !

May Christ be in their eyes that see
   Thy servant, and their ears that hear ;
Christ in his thoughts who thinks on me,
   Christ on his lips who draweth near.

I bind as armour on my breast
   The Threefold Name whereon I call,
Of Father, Son, and Spirit blest,
   The Maker and the Judge of all.

Salvation is of Thee, the Incarnate Word ;
Now and for ever save us, Christ our Lord !

Notes.

ST. PATRICK'S HYMN.

1. The following is the Irish preface to the Hymn found in the Liber Hymnorum, Trinity College, Dublin, folio 196. The translation is given, with the original Irish, on p. 381 of the Rolls *Triparite Life of St. Patrick*. We quote it as a curiosity, and nothing more, not, of course, endorsing the truth of the legend referred to.

'Patrick made this hymn. In the time of Loegaire, son of Niall, it was made. Now, the cause of making it was to protect himself with his monks against the deadly enemies who were in ambush against the clerics. And this is a corslet of faith for the protection of body and soul against devils and human beings and vices. Whosoever shall sing it every day, with pious meditation on God, devils will not stay before him. It will be a safeguard to him against all poison and envy. It will be a defence to him against sudden death. It will be a corslet to his soul after dying. Patrick chanted this when the ambushes were set against him by Loegaire, that he might not go to Tara to sow the faith, so that there they seemed before the liers-in-wait to be wild deer, with a fawn behind them, to wit, Benén. And *Fáed Fiada* ("Deer's Cry") is its name.'

According to the story set forth in the Rolls *Tripartite Life* (p. 48), Patrick, with eight young clerics and Benén, his faithful servant or gillie, sometimes called his 'foster-son' (*Tripartite*, p. 144), passed safely through all the men who were lying in wait for them on the occasion of his visit to Tara. The persons lying in ambush saw only eight deer running away, and a fawn after them, which was Benén.

2. 'The first word of this hymn *Atomriug* was mistaken by Dr. Petrie and Dr. O'Donovan for an obsolete form of the dative of *Temur*, Temoria or Tara, and was by them translated "*At Tara*." We cannot now regret this error, as to it we owe the publication of this curious poem in the *Essay on Tara*. But it is certainly a mistake, and was acknowledged as such by Dr. O'Donovan before his death. The word is a verb ; *ad-domriug*, *i.e.*, *ad-riug*, *adjungo*, with the infixed pronoun *dom*, "to me" (see Zeuss, *Gram. Celt.* p. 336) ; the verb *riug*, which occurs in the forms *ad-riug*, *con-riug*, signifies "to join."' (Dr. Todd's *St. Patrick*, p. 426.) The true analysis of the word was first pointed out by Dr. Whitley Stokes in the *Saturday Review*, September 5, 1857, p. 225.

3. 'Drs. O'Donovan and Petrie translate the original word *togairm*, *invoco*, but it is a substantive, not a verb.' (*Todd*, p. 46.)

4. Dr. Todd thought *cretim* in this line was a noun, but it is obviously the common verb, *i.e.*, the Latin *credo*. The word for 'Threeness' is different from that for 'Trinity,' hence we have followed Dr. Whitley Stokes' new version. The sense is the same as that given in our former edition, 'the faith of the Trinity in Unity,' only fuller in expression. *Fóisin* in this line was rendered by Petrie 'under the.' But the correct reading is *fóisitin*, the instrumental sing. 'with the confession.' (See the Rolls *Tripartite Life*, pp. 48, 650.)

5. The original is *dail*, genitive sing. of *dal*, 'judgment,' 'doom,' as in *dal báis*, 'doom of death,' *Lebor na hUidre*, p. 118 b., not *dúile*, 'elements,' as generally given. (See the Rolls *Tripartite*, pp. 566, 645.) Patrick seems to have had in mind the passage in Isaiah xlv. 7, where the words 'I make peace and create evil' [Vulg. *et creans malum*] are used of God as 'the Creator of judgment.' Comp. Amos iii. 6.

The expression in the Hymn 'the Creator of Judgment' or 'Creator of Doom,' appears to afford an undesigned evidence of the Patrician authorship of the poem. 'God of Judgment' (*dar moDia mbratha*—*Lebar Brecc* in the Rolls *Tripartite*, p. 460) was a favourite expression of Patrick

(compare Isaiah xxx. 18, Malachi ii. 17, *Deus judicii*).
Compare his saying : '*I cannot judge, but God will judge.*'
(Rolls *Tripartite*, p. 288.)   Another expression, '*My
God's doom !*' or '*judgment*' (*mo debrod, mo debroth*), was
constantly in his mouth.   (See the Rolls *Tripartite*, pp.
132, 138, 142, 168, 174, &c.)   It is explained in the
extract from Cormac's Glossary, p. 571.   The thoughts
of the saint, on his way to Tara, must necessarily have
dwelt much on the judgment and doom of idolaters in
'the day of vengeance of our God' (Isa. lxi. 2).   The
Irish for the 'judgment of doom' in the last line of the
second stanza of the Hymn is *brethemnas bratha*.   Hence
we have used a different English word in these places to
express the difference in the original Irish.

6. Dr. Whitley Stokes has throughout 'virtue' in place of
'power.'

7. The original is *grad hiruphin*, which is thus rendered by
Dr. Whitley Stokes.   The former translation was 'the love of
seraphim.'

8. This line is not in the Trinity College Liber Hymnorum.
It is taken from the Bodleian copy.

9. Dr. Todd renders 'in the prayers of the noble fathers.'
Hennessy and Dr. Whitley Stokes, 'patriarchs.'

10. The original has 'in the preachings' of apostles and 'in
the faiths of confessors' in the plural, instead of 'preaching' and
'faith.'

11. So the Bodleian copy.   The Trinity College MS. has
etrochta snechtai, *i.e.*, 'whiteness of snow.'

12. The line was formerly translated 'the force of fire, the
flashing of lightning.

13. Dr. Whitley Stokes would render 'firmness' or 'steadi-
ness of rock.'

14. So Dr. Whitley Stokes.   The former translation was 'to
give me speech.'   Comp. 1 Peter iv. 11.

15. So Dr. Whitley Stokes.   The former version was 'to
prevent me.'

16. The translation of the word 'the lusts' is uncertain, and
consequently there is a blank left here in Dr. Whitley Stokes'
version.

17. So Dr. Whitley Stokes.   The former translation was
'with few or with many,' which gives almost the same sense.

18. Dr. Whitley Stokes has 'I summon to-day all these
virtues between me [and these evils].'   Dr. Todd's translation
is 'I have set around me.'

19. So Dr. Whitley Stokes, as the Irish is *heretecda*.   There

are slight verbal changes in his translation here which are of little importance.

20. Dr. Todd's translation is 'which blinds the soul of man,' the Trinity College MS. saying nothing of man's body (*corp*).

21. So Dr. Whitley Stokes renders. The words are an imitation of Eph. iii. 18, 19, 'That ye being rooted and grounded in love, may be strong to apprehend with all the saints what is the breadth and length and height and depth, and to know the love of Christ which passeth knowledge.' The original in the Trinity College MS. is *Crist illius, Crist issius* [*ipsius* in the Bodleian MS.], *Crist inerus.* Dr. Whitley Stokes, in his *Goidelica* (2nd edit., London, 1872, p. 153), regards *lius* as a derivative of *leth* 'breadth'; *sius* as derived from *sith*, 'long'; and *erus* as a derivative of '*er*,' which is glossed by *uasal.* This Irish gloss is decisive, and shows the reference to be to Eph. iii. The words in the original have not yet been discovered elsewhere in old Irish. The former version was 'Christ in the fort, Christ in the chariot-seat, Christ in the poop,' and was explained to mean: Christ with me when I am at home; Christ with me when I am travelling by land, and in the ship when I am travelling by water. The Irish words were formerly explained: *lius* as dat. sing. of *les*, 'fort'; *sius* as dat. of *ses*, cognate with *suidim*, 'I sit'; *erus* as dat. sing. of *eross*, 'poop.'

22. See note 5.

23. The original of this antiphon is in Latin, the rest of the hymn is in Irish. The last stanza is—

Domini est salus, Domini est salus, Christi est salus,
Salus tua, Domine, sit semper nobiscum.

THE CONFESSION OF PATRICK.

CHAPTER I.

1. This is the title given in three manuscripts. Some have 'the beginning of the Confession of St. Patrick, Bishop.'

2. Patrick or Patricius was a common name among the Romans of Britain. It occurs in Hübner's volume of British Inscriptions in Mommsen's great *Corpus* of Latin Inscriptions, Tom. vii., Nos. 1198 and 1336. Like many persons mentioned in the Scriptures, Patrick had many names. Patrick was his

Roman or Latin name. Tirechan tells us that he had no less than three Celtic names, Succetus [Sucat], Magonus, and Cothraige (Cothrighe). See *Anal. Bolland* ii. 35. (*G. T. Stokes.*) See *Tripartite*, p. 17.

3. According to the *Trip.* the Irish name of Politus was Fotid. Patrick's mother was Concessa, sister of Martin of Tours (so Marianus Scotus). There is, moreover, a citation from a text of the *Confessio*, not now in existence, but quoted in Colgan's *Quarta Vita*, which says, 'I am Patrick, son of Calfurnius, having a mother Conchessa' (Rolls *Trip.*, p. xciii.).

4. Archdeacon Hamilton, partly following the Bollandist text, translates : 'I, Patrick, a most unlearned sinner, the least of all the faithful, and the most contemptible amongst many, have had for my father Calphurnius, a deacon, who was the son of Potitus, formerly a priest.' The construing of '*rusticissimus*' with '*peccator*' is faulty ; but the translation of the next clause is more so. The Bollandist text has 'filium quondam Potiti Presbyteri,' rendered by Hamilton '*son of Potitus, formerly a priest.*' The order of the words proves, however, that Nicholson's translation of that text is correct : '*the son of the late Potitus, a presbyter.*' Olden adopts that reading. The reading of the Book of Armagh is, however, probably correct : 'filium quendam Potiti [filii Odissi] presbyteri,' lit. '*a certain son of Potitus, a presbyter.*' The words in brackets are written in the margin of the Armagh copy. If the word 'presbyteri' be referred to Odissus, the Confession would contradict the statement of Fiacc's hymn, according to which Patrick is described as 'son of Calpurn, son of Potitus, grandson of Deacon Odisse.' If we combine the two statements, St. Patrick's parents up to the third generation must have been clergymen. In his summary of the Life of St. Patrick, Hamilton remarks, 'His father's name was Calphurnius ; he was a Decurion, and had been formerly a deacon. I say formerly, because the law of ecclesiastical celibacy being then, as now, in force, his acceptation of Holy Orders was in conformity with this law.' Hamilton here confuses what is said of the father with what is recorded of the grandfather. But even thus the passage is against clerical celibacy. The Archdeacon is, however, more honest than the Very Rev. Arthur Ryan, of Thurles, who, in his *St. Patrick, Apostle of Ireland*, ignores the entire statement as to St. Patrick's ecclesiastical progenitors, stating that 'his father Calphurnius was, the saint tells us, a Roman officer of good family.' This is a *suppressio veri* with a vengeance.

St. Patrick was proud of his noble birth and of his Roman descent. Compare his remark, the *Epistle to Coroticus*, § 5, p. 76, and one of the 'sayings' on p. 84. This makes the fact more remarkable that he nowhere alludes to any commission received from Rome.

5. Variously spelled in the MSS. Banavem or Benaven.

6. The birthplace of Patrick has been the subject of a prolonged controversy. Scotland, France, Ireland, have each had their champions. The claim of Ireland may be at once dismissed. It is grounded on a paragraph in the *Epistle to Coroticus* (p. 78), where he identifies himself with his injured converts and disciples, and protests against the Welsh invaders : 'with them it is a crime that we have been born in Hibernia.' In other parts of his writings he equally clearly asserts that he was not an Irishman by birth. As to the claim of France, some have upheld Boulogne as his natal place. This is possible, for, as is shown in note 6, the predatory expeditions of Niall of the Nine Hostages extended to that port during the boyhood and youth of our Saint. The majority of critics now uphold the claim of Dumbarton. Dumbarton in ancient times was called *Alclut*, [old Welsh, *Ail cluaithe* in old Irish], and formed the western termination of the Roman Wall extending from the Forth to the Clyde. That wall was constructed by Agricola about the year 80 A.D., and renewed in the second century under Antoninus Pius. Dumbarton, with its great rock as an acropolis, formed a natural stronghold and post of observation against the Scotic freebooters of the Antrim coast. The Romans, though they never settled in Ireland, yet made the acquaintance of the Irish. Agricola even in the first century contemplated the conquest of the island, and with that design entertained a fugitive Irish prince, as Tacitus tells us. The Romans of Dumbarton must have suffered much at the hands of Irish pirates down to the fifth century, as is testified by the numerous finds of Roman coins all along the Antrim coast. (See *Ireland and the Celtic Church*, p. 16, where I discuss this point and refer to *Proceedings of Royal Irish Academy*, vol. ii. 184–190 ; v. 199 ; vi. 442, 525 ; John Scott Porter in the *Ulster Journal of Archæology*, 1854, pp. 182–191 ; and Hübner's *Brit. Ins.* in *Corp. Ins. Lat.* tom. vii., p. 221, No. 1198.) As soon as the Romans abandoned Britain, the Antrim Celts established the kingdom of Dalriada, in Argyleshire, which became the root out of which sprang the mediæval kingdom of Scotland. (*G. T. Stokes*.)

7. The Book of Armagh says, 'villulam enim prope habuit ubi ego capturam dedi.' In the Bollandist edition it is ' villam enim (Enon) prope habuit ubi ego in capturam decidi.' Archdeacon Hamilton incorrectly renders this 'near the village of Enon where I was made captive.' If the reading of the Bollandist copy be correct, we might conjecture that St. Patrick's

father gave the name Enon to his farm because of its abundance
of water (comp. John iii. 23).

8. The date of Patrick's first captivity cannot be exactly
determined, but the known facts of history all coincide with his
own statements. The last half of the fourth century was marked
by continual ravages of the English coasts by the Picts and Scots,
or Irish, as the word Scot in those days always signified. Am-
mianus Marcellinus the historian, and the poet Claudian were
contemporaries of the incursions. They both testify to the
vigour with which the Irish desolated the English coasts. In
A.D. 343 they began the conflict. In A.D. 360 they kept
possession of a great portion of Britain for ten years, till over-
thrown and repelled by Theodosius, the most celebrated Roman
general of the day, in A.D. 369. On this occasion the Irish were
commanded by an Irish king named Crimthann. Claudian the
poet speaks of ' Icy Ierne,' weeping for the heaps of those slain
in that campaign. The *Annals of the Four Masters* tell us that
in A.D. 405, Niall of the Nine Hostages was slain at Boulogne,
after a life spent in such ravages. See Keating's *History of Ireland*,
ed. O'Mahony, pp. 369–390 ; Ussher's *Works*, vi. 116. (*G. T.
Stokes*.)

9. Compare what St. Patrick says here as to his ignorance of
God in the days of his youth with the similar statement made
in the end of this chapter at p. 50, that he was ' like a stone
lying in deep mud,' and with the more detailed account of his
irreligion, § 12, p. 58, and § 15, p. 61. These statements are
in direct contradiction to the legendary stories which make him
out a marvel of sanctity and a worker of miracles from his very
infancy.

10. The Latin is here ' sacerdotibus nostris.'

11. The phrase seems taken from 2 Chron. xxix. 10, where,
however, the Vulgate Latin has *furorem iræ suæ*, in place of the
words quoted by Patrick, *iram animationis suæ*, which, however,
agree in sense with the Vulgate. The Itala rendering of the
passage in 2 Chron. is not extant. Hennessy and others have,
however, translated the phrase ' the anger of His Spirit.'

12. Archdeacon Hamilton has ' amongst the Gentiles.' The
Latin is simply ' in gentibus multis,' which does not convey that
idea.

13. Lat. ' parvitas mea.' Archdeacon Hamilton, somewhat too
strongly, ' my unworthiness.'

14. Lat. ' sensum incredulitatis meæ ' (*Book of Armagh*). The
Bollandists have ' sensum incredulitatis cordis mei.' Archdeacon
Hamilton, freely, ' the ears of my incredulous heart.'

15. So Dr. Whitley Stokes reads *ut converterem*   The

Cottonian MS. (*converterer*) is 'and that I might be converted.'
The Armagh MS. is *ut confirmarem*, 'that I might strengthen.'

16. Archdeacon Hamilton, too freely, 'had compassion on the
ignorance of my youth.' Our translation is literal.

17. The Cottonian MS. has 'admonished.' So the Bollandists
whom Hamilton has followed.

18. Patrick had evidently here in his mind, as may be seen
from the Latin, the passage in Psa. cvii. 15 (cvi. 15, *Douay
Version*), *Confiteantur . . . mirabilia ejus.* The Vulg. and the
Itala here are alike.

19. Lat. 'præter Deum Patrem ingenitum.' Not as Hamilton,
'*except* our unbegotten God, the Father.'

20. The Armagh MS. has *inerrabiliter*, which means 'unerr-
ingly,' but as Prof. O'Mahony suggested, and the suggestion is
adopted by Hennessy, it was probably intended for *inenarrabiliter*,
which is the reading of the Bodleian MS., 'ineffably,' or 'inex-
plicably.' Sir S. Ferguson translates : ' in wise unspeakable.'

21. The words 'and invisible' are omitted in the Book of
Armagh.

22. According to the Armagh MS. the sentence reads 'death
having been vanquished, in the heavens.' But the text is
evidently defective. The Cottonian and Bodleian MSS. and the
Bollandist have as above.

23. 'And under the earth,' Lat. 'et infernorum,' as in the
Vulgate, which is translated in the Douay 'and under the
earth.' Hence our version. Hamilton has 'and in hell.' After
the words, 'above every name,' the words, 'that in the name of
Jesus every knee shall bow,' are inserted in brackets by Whitley
Stokes without any note as to the MS. which gives that addition.
Olden inserts them in his translation. But they are omitted in
the Cottonian MS. and in the Bollandist text, and it would seem
also in the Armagh MS.

24. 'To Him' is added in the Book of Armagh. We have
marked with inverted commas the portions of the verses quoted
(Phil. ii. 9–11) which agree with the Vulgate, and are translated
in the Douay. The text, as a whole, differs from both the
Vulgate and the Itala. Some MSS. follow the Vulgate in the
last clause, reading : 'that the Lord Jesus Christ is in the glory
of God the Father.'

25. Rom. ii. 6. Patrick agrees substantially with the Vulgate,
which has *opera ejus ;* Patrick, ungrammatically, *facta sua.*

26. So the text should be rendered : ' *et effudit in nobis habunde
Spiritum Sanctum donum et pignus immortalitatis.*' The first part
of this sentence is taken from Titus iii. 6, with the ungrammatical
alteration of *in nobis* instead of *in nos.*

27. The Bollandists add 'the Father,' followed naturally by Hamilton.

28. The Creed of Patrick differs in form from the Nicene Creed, so does the Irish Creed found in the Antiphonary of Bangor, reprinted in O'Laverty's *Diocese of Down and Connor.* In the fourth century the forms of the Creed varied very much. The early custom of preserving the creeds by memory alone tended to increase such variations. (*G. T. Stokes.*)

29. Psa. l. 15 (Psa. xlix. 15, *Douay Version*). Patrick's quotation is not from the Vulgate Version, though there is no substantial difference made thereby in the sense of the passage. The Itala is nearer Patrick's text, reading *et magnificabis me*, but it also differs from Patrick, for it has *eripiam* for *liberabo.*

30. Tobit xii. 7. The quotation is identical with the passage in the Vulgate.

31. Lat. 'scire qualitatem meam.' Hamilton renders too freely, 'should be made acquainted with my circumstances.'

32. Psa. v. 6 (Psa. v. 7, *Douay Version*). In the Vulgate the word 'all' is found in place of 'those.' The Itala here agrees with Patrick. Some MSS. of Patrick agree with the Vulgate.

33. Some MSS. omit 'says in the Gospel.'

34. Matthew xii. 36. The Vulgate and Itala correctly, following the original Greek, have 'every idle word.' So Hamilton ; but the text of St. Patrick is as in our translation.

35. The Book of Armagh has 'Domini Christi.' The Bollandists read, 'Domini nostri Jesu Christi,' which Hamilton follows.

36. That is, 'I feared their censure.' So Sir S. Ferguson, and Archdeacon Hamilton, 'I feared I would encounter the reproaches of men.' The clause has, however, been explained otherwise. Dr. Whitley Stokes renders in a note : 'I feared offending against (doing violence to) the language of men,' *i.e.*, that I could not express myself like others.

37. We have followed here Sir S. Ferguson's translation—

> Who, excellently versed in civic law,
> And sacred letters, in a like degree.

The original is ungrammatical, and therefore obscure. O'Conor supposed the 'in both ways' to refer to the knowledge of both the Greek original and the Latin Version, and so Nicholson. The Armagh MS. has 'quia non dedici sicut et cæteri qui optime itaque 'jure et sacras literas utroque pari modo combiberunt et sermones illorum ex infantia numquam motarunt.' The Bollandists have quin non legi, sicut cæteri qui optime sacris litteris sunt

imbuti, et studium suum ex infantia nunquam mutaverunt,'
which appears to be a correction of the original, and which
Hamilton translates freely, ' not being educated as others, who
were very learned in the sacred Scriptures, and who have never
changed their studious condition since infancy.'

38. That is, his Latin was always growing worse by his being
obliged constantly to speak in Irish.

39. *Ex salive (saliva) scripturæ meæ.* Hamilton, incorrectly,
' from the context of my writing.'

40. So, after Sir S. Ferguson, we render *in sermonibus.* Nicholson
translates ' in languages.' Hennessy has ' in speech.' Hamilton
' in my conversations.'

41. Ecclesiasticus iv. 29. The Vulgate and Itala are somewhat
fuller here : ' For by the tongue wisdom is discerned, and understanding and knowledge and learning by the word of the wise.'
(*Douay Version.*) The last clause in the Vulgate is *et doctrina in
verbo sensati.* Some MSS. read *varietatis,* ' of variety,' in place of
veritatis.

42. That is, what use is it to plead my deficiencies when I have
still the presumption to become an author in spite of them ? The
Book of Armagh has ' sed quid prodest excussatio,' &c. The
Bollandist text omits *quid,* though it preserves the interrogation
at end. Hamilton, not regarding the latter, renders ' but defence
is profitable if true, especially when one has anything to presume
upon.'

43. The Bollandists and the Cottonian MS. read, ' my sins prevented me,' and so Hamilton. The meaning is as Olden translates, ' circumstances prevented me.' In the end of the sentence
the Cottonian MS. reads, ' quod ante non perlegeram.' The
insertion of the *non* is incorrect, though adopted by Olden.

44. That is, scarcely above childish language. So the Armagh
MS., the Bodleian MS., and the Bollandist, *puer in verbis.*
Nicholson reads, after the Cottonian MS., *puer imberbis,* ' a
beardless boy ; ' and so Hamilton.

45. The clause *vel quid adpeterem* is omitted by Nicholson, and
passed over by Hennessy.

46. We follow here the Cottonian MS., correcting, with Dr.
Whitley Stokes, *desertis* into *disertus.*

47. The original can scarcely be rendered as Sir S. Ferguson—

> With brevity and elegance of speech,
> To treat deep things, as, how the Spirit moves,
> The soul's affections, and the human mind.

For the original of the latter clause is : *Sicut enim spiritus gestit*

9

et animas (animus) et sensus monstrat adfectus. Hennessy renders :
' as the spirit desires, and the mind and intellect point out,' but
that rendering ignores *adfectus.*

48. The reference is to Isa. xxxii. 4, where the Latin Vulgate,
following the Hebrew, has 'and the tongue of stammerers shall
speak readily (*velociter*) and plain.' (*Douay Version.*) The Itala
is nearer to Patrick, *linguæ balbutientium cito discent loqui pacem.*
Hamilton corrects the quotation after the Vulgate.

49. The text quoted is 2 Cor. iii. 3. It is substantially, but
not verbally, the same as the Vulgate, which has ' written in our
hearts.'

50. Ecclus. vii. 16. Patrick evidently understood by *rusticatio*
' rural life,' with the want of learning which generally accompanies
it. Hence Sir S. Ferguson renders the word ' unlearning.'
Hamilton renders ' simplicity,' forgetful of the sense of the
passage in Eccles. vii.

51. Nicholson and others read as above, following the Cottonian
MS., and the Bollandists who read *in summo pariete.* Hennessy,
after the Armagh MS., reads *in sua parte,* ' in His part.'

52. *Vos dominicati,* which is the reading of the Armagh MS.,
is rendered by Sir S. Ferguson, ' you lords of the land.' But Dr.
Whitley Stokes prefers the reading of the Bodleian MS., *et vos
Domini ignari rethorici.* Hennessy renders ' and ye of the Lord.'
Nicholson reads *et vos ignari Domini,* 'and ye ignorant of the
Lord,' and so the Bollandists.

53. The Cottonian MS. adds ' I should serve ' (*prodessem*).
The verb is omitted in the Armagh MS.

54. The Armagh reading is *si vivus fuero,* ' as long as I shall
live.' But Dr. Whitley Stokes reads, after the Cottonian MS.,
si dignus fuero, which is given in the margin of the Book of
Armagh.

55. Instead of ' et naturaliter deservirem illis,' which is the reading of the Book of Armagh, the Cottonian MS. has the adverb
' veraciter,' and the Bollandists read the whole passage, 'et veraciter.
deservirem illi in mensura.' The clause is translated freely from
the latter text by Archdeacon Hamilton. ' Finally, that in all
humility and truth I should serve Him [Christ] without end
or measure.'

CHAPTER II.

1. The Book of Armagh and the Cottonian MS. commence
this paragraph with ' *in mensura,*' which phrase the Bollandist edition
connects with the close of the preceding chapter. See note there.

2. *Exgallias,* usually explained as 'Gallican,' but Sir S. Ferguson renders it as above, and so Dr. Whitley Stokes explains it as *exægallias,* 'legacies,' 'patterns,' pp. 361, 673.

2*b.* The Book of Armagh and Cottonian MS. have '*post erumnas et tantas moles,*' the Bollandist, '*post ærumnas tantæ molis.*' Hence Hamilton's translation, 'after so many changes of such magnitude.'

3. The Latin is *pecora,* the meaning of which is doubtful. According to the *Tripartite Life,* Patrick was employed feeding swine.

4. Patrick's place of captivity was close to the village of Broughshane, five miles from Ballymena. He lived in a valley near the Hill of Slemish, now called the Valley of the Braid, from the river which flows through it. There is a townland in the valley still called Ballyligpatrick, or the town of Patrick's Hollow. In this are still some remains of an Irish chieftain's rath, or fort. See Reeves' *Antiquities of Down and Connor,* pp. 83, 84. (*G. T. Stokes.*)

5. There was a frequent commerce by ships between Ireland and France in those early centuries. Columbanus in the sixth century was placed on board a ship of Nantes, bound for Ireland, by order of Queen Brunehault. Bishop Arculf, about A.D. 690, escaped from Iona in a ship which traded to France. See *Ireland and the Celtic Church,* pp. 99, 142. (*G. T. Stokes.*)

6. Lat. *intermissi hominem.* Hamilton renders, '*met the man,*' but such a rendering does not suit the context.

7. This was Milchu, son of Hua Bain, King of North Dalaradia. There were two districts of Antrim, one called Dalriada, now corrupted into the word Route, embracing the glens of Antrim ; another called Dalaradia, forming the centre of the county. Milchu is said to have burned himself to death when Patrick came to preach the gospel to him. See the Patrician History in the Book of Armagh, as printed in the *Analecta Bollandiana,* i. 559, by Rev. E. Hogan, S.J. (*G. T. Stokes.*)

8. Hamilton has, 'and in the power of God, he directed my course till I came to Benum.' But, according to the Bollandist text, the '*in virtute Dei*' should be connected with the '*veni ad Benum.*' Upon this name many theories have been raised as to the special locality where Patrick took ship. All the MSS., however, including the Book of Armagh, the Cottonian, and Bodleian, read *ad bonum,* which is translated in our text. Sir S. Ferguson compares the Irish expression *go maith.*

9. So the Book of Armagh, reading *ut abirem unde navigarem,* but the Cottonian MS. has *ut haberem unde navigarem,* which would mean, 'I told them that I had the wherewith to sail with them,' that is, that I could pay for my passage. Hamilton

translates the Bollandist text, 'I asked for the means to set sail.'
The probability is that Patrick told his dream to the sailors in
order to induce the captain to take him on board.

10. So Bodleian MS., reading *cum indignatione*. The Book of
Armagh reads *cum interrogatione*.

11. The Book of Armagh and the Cottonian MS. have '*quia
ex fide recipimus te.*' The Bollandists have '*quia ex fide reperimus
te,*' which Hamilton translates, 'Come, for we have found thee
faithful.'

12. The original is *itaque reppuli sugere* (Gilbert reads *fugere*)
mammellas eorum. Dr. Whitley Stokes (pp. 362, 666) compares
Isa. lx. 16. This is, however, scarcely possible, though supported
by Olden. The Cottoni an MS. reads *itaque repuli fugere,* omitting
the rest of the sentence. The Bollandist has *et in illa die debui
surgere in navem eorum propter Deum,* but in the note it adds that
the MS. had *repuli sugere mammas eorum.* The Bodleian MS. has
itaque repulis fugire mammas. Archdeacon Hamilton's translation,
based upon the Bollandist edition, is not very clear. It is thus
rendered and punctuated : 'Upon that day I entered their ship.
On account of God, nevertheless, I had no hopes that they would
say to me, "Come to us in the faith of Christ," because they were
Gentiles.' The Latin *gentes* is evidently used in this passage in
the sense of *heathen.*

13. We have followed Sir S. Ferguson's rendering. It is difficult to understand what is meant by the Latin *et ob hoc obtinui cum
illis,* which gives no sense when rendered literally. Hennessy
paraphrases : 'and this I obtained from them.' The other translations depart more widely from the text.

14. The Armagh MS. omits 'and we sailed immediately.'

15. The Bollandist edition has *twenty-seven,* Hamilton's *thirty-
seven* is probably a mere typographical mistake. Compare this
statement about the twenty-eight days' journey through a desert
with that in second paragraph of chap. iii. p. 56. The two
accounts seem somewhat mixed up together.

16. The life and writings of Gregory of Tours clearly prove
that Paganism extensively prevailed in Gaul between A.D. 400
and 600. Even amongst Christians their conversion was very
imperfect. Many Pagan customs even still survive in our midst
It was the same in the East. In the sixth century a strong Pagan
party still existed in Constantinople, some interesting notices of
which are to be found in the *Ecclesiastical History* of John of
Ephesus, translated from the Syriac by Dr. R. Payne Smith,
Dean of Canterbury. (*G. T. Stokes.*)

17. Other MSS. 'with faith and the whole heart.'

18. The words 'this day' are not in Hennessy's text, which

gives the Armagh reading, but they are in the Cottonian and Bollandist texts. In the sentence following the Bollandists have *nobis* and *in viam nostram*, which is expressed in Hamilton's translation.

19. Hamilton incorrectly, ' until we are comforted.'

20. The words 'fainted and ' are supplied from the Cottonian MS.

21. The Book of Armagh omits ' from that day forth they had food in abundance ;' but the words are found in the Bollandist text, and in the Cottonian and Bodleian MSS.

22. In the Brussels codex of Muirchu's Life of St. Patrick there is a strange construction put upon this statement which shows how easily the simplest story can be transformed into the miraculous. ' But the holy Patrick tasting nothing of this food, for it was offered in sacrifice, being neither hungry nor thirsty, remained unharmed.' See Hogan's *Analecta Bollandiana*, tom. i., and the Rolls *Tripartite*, p. 494. The sequel of the story shows, however, plainly that Patrick did suffer from partaking of the pork after his long hunger, and had a nightmare in consequence of that repast.

23. It is evident from the context that Satan is here the subject of the verb, and therefore that the passage should be rendered as in our text. Hamilton renders it, ' for there fell upon me as it were, a huge piece of rock.'

24. We have followed here substantially Sir S. Ferguson's translation. He connects the words *et nihil membrorum prævalens sed unde mihi venit in spiritum*, observing that the Latin *sed* is used after the analogy of the Irish *acht* as equivalent to *nisi*, a usage elsewhere found in the *Confessio*.

25. *Helias* has been explained by Dr. Todd as equivalent to *Eli*, the Hebrew for 'my God,' which occurs in the Gospel account of the Crucifixion, Matt. xxvii. 45 ; Mark xv. 34. Others, as Probus, the author of the Fifth Life of Patrick, consider the word to have been the Greek Helios, ' the sun,' and that Patrick ' invoked Christ, the true Sun.' *Helios* and *Helias* were associated at an early period (see *Whitley Stokes*, p. 669). Others, with Jocelin, explain the passage to mean that Patrick invoked the aid of the prophet Elias or Elijah ; but that is far-fetched. The contrast between the sun and Christ is alluded to in the end of the *Confession*, p. 71.

26. Some MSS. *Helias! Helias!*

27. The words 'I was aided' and 'His Spirit was then' are omitted in the Armagh MS., but they are found in other MSS., and are needed to complete the sense.

28. Matt. x. 20. There are unimportant variations here in the MSS. Some do not give the whole verse.

1. Sir S. Ferguson maintains that the Latin *iterum post annos multos adhuc capturam dedi ea noĉte prima*, especially the use of *adhuc*, 'still,' shows that these words are necessarily to be understood of a spiritual captivity, a captivity still continuing. 'It was the first occasion on which he had experienced what he conceived to be the presence of an indwelling coercer of his will, to obedience to whose promptings all his subsequent life was to be conformed.' (*Ferguson*, pp. 113, 114.) Others consider a second aĉtual captivity to be here referred to. Hamilton translates 'I was again made captive by the Gentiles,' but the words 'by the Gentiles' are not in any of the MSS.

2. The Armagh MS. omits 'saying to me.'

3. Some MSS. 'we came to men,' reading *ad homines*, instead of *omnes*, which is followed by Olden.

4. Some MSS. read here also *ad homines* for *omnes*.

5. The order of the first two paragraphs is reversed in the Bollandist edition, where the second paragraph of our chap. iii. is placed at the end of chap. ii.

6. 'Amongst the Britons': *in Britannis*, as in the Irish gloss on Fiacc, *in bretna:b*. (*Sir S. Ferguson*.) Patrick wrote 'in the Britains.' This was striĉtly accurate, and is an interesting little proof of the genuineness of our document. The correĉt designation among the Romans for Britain was *Britanniæ*, because it was divided in the fourth century, the age of Patrick's youth, into five provinces ; *Britannia Prima, Britann:a Secunda, Maxima Cæsariensis, Flav:a Cæsariensis*, and *Valentia* the fifth province. The last was organised by Theodosius after he repelled the Irish invaders. It comprised the extreme northern portion of the Roman dominions and embraced South-western Scotland. (*G. T. Stokes.*)

7. *The wood of Foclut.* The wood here mentioned by Patrick was, as Mr. Olden has noted, situated in and near the parish of Killala, barony of Tirawley, and county of Mayo. Compare the remarks of the Rev. E. Hogan, S.J., in his *Analeĉta Bollandiana*, ii. 42, and O'Donovan's *Hy-Fiachrach*, pp. 463, 464. (*G. T. Stokes.*)

8. 'As if with one voice,' is omitted in the Book of Armagh.

9. The Bollandist edition has *in me, an juxta me verbis peritissimis and:cbam quosdam ex spiritu ʃ sallentes intra me, et nesciebam qui essent quos andivi:* 'I heard within me, or beside me, some persons singing from the spirit within me the most eloquent words, and I knew not who they were whom I heard.' But this reading does not agree with the close of the passage in which the singular is used as in our translation. Archdeacon

Hamilton has in his translation rendered the latter words in the plural. But this is not in accordance with the Bollandist text. The plural *quos* before *audivi* is found in some MSS., but not the phrase *ex spiritu psallentes intra me*.

10. The Bollandist edition omits the words 'is He who speaks in thee' (*ipse est qui loquitur in te*). And so consequently Hamilton.

11. The phrase 'full of joy' (*gaudibundus*) is omitted in the Bollandist edition, and so by Hamilton.

12. The Bollandists read *audivi*, 'I heard,' instead of *vidi*, 'I saw,' as in the other MSS.

13. Hennessy and Gilbert, with Cottonian and other MSS., read *eram*. Dr. Whitley Stokes, with the Bollandists, has *erat*.

14. The Armagh MS. omits 'above me.'

15. Lat. *super interiorem hominem*, not 'within my inner man,' as Hamilton.

16. The Bollandists have *dixit se esse spiritum*, rendered by Hamilton '*he said he was a spirit*.' It ought to be *the Spirit*. The Armagh and other MSS. '*sic effatus est ut sit eps,*' i.e., *episcopus*. Others have *sps*., *spiritus*. These contractions are easily, as Dr. Todd says, confounded in the MSS. If the former be the true reading, the meaning seems to be that he spoke with authority as the great 'bishop of souls' (1 Pet. ii. 25). The reference must be either to *Christ* or the *Spirit*.

17. The quotation is from Rom. viii. 26, and agrees with the Vulgate and Douay, save that the expression 'the infirmities of our prayers' (some MSS. have the sing. 'infirmity') is used instead of 'our infirmity.'

18. Or 'which I cannot express in words.' So Bollandists.

19. Probably a quotation compounded from 1 John ii. 1, and Rom. viii. 34.

20. This paragraph, with the first paragraph of § 12 and the two first lines of the second, which we have placed within brackets, are not found in the Book of Armagh, but are contained in the Cottonian MS., the Bollandist, and the Bodleian texts.

21. The Latin is *quia necdum prevalebam*, which Hamilton incorrectly translates 'for as yet I had no understanding.'

22. We have followed the Cottonian MS. in connecting *et quotidie* with the preceding sentence, and making the new sentence commence with *contra* used as an adverb. Hamilton, closely following the Bollandist edition (which here agrees with the Cottonian, the passage not being in the Book of Armagh, see note 20), translates 'and daily proceeded, though not willingly, towards Ireland, until I nearly fainted away.' But the passage so punctuated affords no good sense.

23. Hamilton refers to Rom. viii. 28, which is a good reference, although there is no quotation here made from that passage.

24. Lat. *a memoratis superdictis*, which Hamilton renders '*by my above-mentioned censors.*'

25. So Sir S. Ferguson would render the Latin *contra faciem* as being equivalent to the Irish *in agaid*.

26. Some MSS. 'divine response.' And so Hamilton translates 'an answer from the Lord.'

27. So MSS. and the Bollandist edition, but the Armagh MS. reads *audivimus*, which is opposed to the *male vidimus* in the following clause. *Male* is generally rendered 'with displeasure.' Sir S. Ferguson points out that Facciolati gives examples of the phrase in the sense of 'to be ill-styled.' Archdeacon Hamilton translates the sentence, 'we have imperfectly seen the face of him who was marked out to us, and whose name was discovered,' thus rendering *male* by 'imperfectly,' and so in the following sentences.

28. That is 'of the Bishop-designate.' The 'name stripped' of honour means, according to the Bollandists, without any title of honour or mark of episcopal dignity.

29. Zech. ii. 8. The quotation is slightly different from the Vulgate version, and also from the Itala.

30. 'In myself' is inserted by the Cottonian and Bodleian MSS.

31. The Bollandist edition omits *hic et in futurum*, 'now or for the future.'

32. The three paragraphs that follow to the end of the chapter are enclosed in brackets, because wanting in the Book of Armagh. They occur in the Cottonian MS. and other MSS.

33. Lat. *ante defensionem illam*, which Hamilton strangely renders, 'before such prohibition.'

34. 'In the Britains.' See note 6, p. 134.

35. Cottonian MS., *pro me pulsaret ;* Bollandist edition *pulsetur pro me.*

35*b.* The Cottonian MS. reads *audenter;* Sir S. Ferguson *audienter*, which he translates 'audibly.' The adverb is omitted in the Bollandist text and in the Book of Armagh.

36. The Latin is 'ita ut hodie confidenter offeram illi sacrificium ut hostiam viventem animam meam Christo Domino meo.' The reference is to Rom. xii. 1, as is seen by the Latin *hostiam viventem*, which occurs in Patrick's original and in the Itala and Vulg. Archdeacon Hamilton translates obscurely, 'so that daily, with confidence, I offer sacrifice to him, and consecrate my soul a living victim to my Lord.'

37. 2 Sam. vii. 18 (2 Kings vii. 18, *Douay Version*).

38. Or 'calling' (1 Cor. i. 26). The Latin is '*quæ est vocatio mea?*' Hamilton renders 'What is my dessert?'

39. The Cottonian MS. has *qui mihi tantam divinitatem cooper-*

uisti. The Bollandist reading is *qui mihi tantam divinitatem denudasti.* Hamilton's rendering is 'that you should have showered such graces on me.'

40. The Bollandist edition omits the words '*in gentibus constanter,*' which are therefore not in Hamilton's translation.

41. There seems to be a reference here to Rom. xv. 9.

42. We here followed Sir S. Ferguson in supposing *indubitabilem eum* to refer to God. So Hamilton, who renders it by 'faithful.' Hennessy refers it to Patrick, rendering 'undoubtedly'; so Olden, and similarly Nicholson, who loosely renders the clause: 'That I should place no bounds to my trust in Him.'

43. Hamilton has accidentally omitted to translate the words '*et qui me audierit,*' which are found in the Bollandist as well as in the Cottonian copy.

44. Matt. xxiv. 14. The clause 'before the end of the world' does not agree with the Itala or Vulg. versions.

45. Here ends the portion noticed in note 20, as not found in the Book of Armagh.

CHAPTER IV.

1. The Armagh MS. has *pissimus,* as Gilbert and Whitley Stokes give it. Nicholson, after the Bollandists, *piissimus,* which Hamilton renders 'God of piety,' and so Olden. Possibly the true reading of the Armagh MS. is *p.issimus,* i.e., *potentissimus.* So Sir S. Ferguson seems to have read, for he renders the word 'Almighty.'

2. Lat. *ex duodecim periculis.* Hamilton renders freely 'from the many dangers.' Olden illustrates the expression by quoting the following from the Irish Nennius, p. 112, 'Like seven to the Hebrews, twelve was to the Britons, the absolute number significant of perfection, plenitude, and completeness.'

3. The two paragraphs following, to the end of the first paragraph of § 16, are enclosed in brackets, because they are omitted in the Book of Armagh.

4. The Latin is *ut me pauperculum pupillum* (the Bollandists have *pauperculum et pussilum pupillum*) *ideo tamen* (Bollandists omit *ideo tamen*) *responsum divinum creberrime admoneret.* Hamilton, much too freely, 'admonished me, a poor wretched creature, by his divine revelations.'

5. Psa. xxxix. 4 (Psa. xxxviii. 5, *Douay Version*).

6. There seems to be a reference here to 1 Cor. xv. 10, but it is not absolutely certain.

7. The Bollandist edition has *non ego, sed Dei gratia,* and therefore Hamilton, '*not I, but the grace of God,*' and so Olden.

8. Lat. *ut andirem opprobrium peregrinationis meæ*. Hamilton renders much too freely, 'I heard them upbraid me as a stranger.'

9. Lat. *et ut darem ingenuitatem meam*. Hamilton incorrectly, 'and yet I gave myself up without reserve.' St. Patrick several times alludes to his noble birth and his Roman ancestors, of whom he seems to have been proud. See *Confession*, chap. i. 1, and *Epistle to Coroticus*, § 5, p. 76.

10. Here end the brackets noted in note 3. The closing words of the paragraph are in Latin, *si Dominus indulgeret*, incorrectly rendered by Hamilton, 'if the Lord should demand it.' St. Patrick both anticipated and longed for his martyrdom, which proves that the legends are wrong which relate that he converted all Ireland. See *Confession*, chap. v. §§ 23, 24, pp. 69, 70.

11. Several MSS. add 'and afterwards consummated,' *i.e.*, confirmed. Hamilton translates, 'and be afterwards perfected.' But the words are not found in the Book of Armagh.

12. Jer. xvi. 19. 'To thee the Gentiles shall come from the ends of the earth.' The words, 'from the ends of the earth,' are not in the Book of Armagh, and the clauses are there inverted. The passage is somewhat shorter in the Bollandist edition followed by Hamilton. The text quoted does not agree in words with the Vulgate, nor generally with the Itala, which is, however, nearer to Patrick's quotation, translating *quam falsa possederunt patres nostri simulachra et non est in eis utilitas*.

13. The text here is almost identical with that in Acts xiii. 47, which is quoted from Isa. xlix. 6.

14. Matt. viii. 11. The Book of Armagh adds, after 'west,' 'and from the south and from the north.'

15. Some MSS. omit the words 'as we believe,' &c.

16. Jer. xvi. 16. The Armagh MS. omits 'he says by the prophets.' It adds after 'the Lord' the words *et cetera*.

17. Matt. xxviii. 19, 20. The Book of Armagh omits verse 20, but inserts the word *reliqua*, which intimates that the latter verse was in the copy which the scribe had before him. See the Rolls *Tripartite*, p. 369.

18. Mark xvi. 15, 16. Some MSS. omit the last clause, and by the Bollandists, which edition Hamilton translates from.

19. Matt. xxiv. 14. (See note 44, chap. iii.) The Book of Armagh adds here 'the rest are examples,' which Sir S. Ferguson is correct in regarding as a note by the scribe, indicating abridgment from a fuller text. So Dr. Whitley Stokes. The Book of Armagh omits all onward to the end of the section.

20. The Bollandist edition omits the clause, 'and your sons shall see visions,' and so Hamilton.

21. Rom. ix. 25, 26, where the Apostle quotes from Hosea (Oσεε) i. 9, 10.

22. Lat. *unde autem Hiberione.* Hamilton freely, 'and now with regard to the Irish.'

23. It has been already noted (note 8, chap. i.), that the word Scot always meant Irishman in these early ages. It was only in the twelfth century that it was finally transferred from the inhabitants of Ireland to those of Scotland. The mistake still lingers on, notwithstanding the efforts of scholars. An amusing incident of its prevalence occurred of late years. That eminent Celtic scholar, Mr. W. M. Hennessy, M.R.I.A., published an ancient Irish book of Annals composed at Clonmacnois, about A.D. 1100, styled *Chronicon Scotorum.* It appeared in the *English Rolls Series,* and is the only one of that series which is now out of print. This occurred through the fervid patriotism of modern Scotchmen, who purchased it, believing it to be a Scottish and not an Irish history. See on this common error Ussher's preface to his *Sylloge Epist. Hib.,* and his *Eccless. Britan. Antiqq.,* cap. xvi., *Works,* vol. vi. p. 276, 281, cf. p. 112 ; Skene's *Celtic Scotland,* i. pp. 137, 398 ; Keating's *History of Ireland,* O'Mahony's edit., p. 375 ; Bishop Reeves, *Proceedings of Royal Irish Acad.* viii. 29 ; Colgan's *Trias Thaumat.,* p. 109. (*G. T. Stokes.*)

24. Guasacht, son of Milchu, the chieftain whose slave Patrick was, became first bishop of Granard in Longford. He is commemorated in the *Martyrology of Donegal,* on January 24th. Milchu's two daughters became consecrated virgins. There is a very curious account of the conversion by Patrick of the daughter of King Laoghaire (Leary). It is preserved in the Book of Armagh. [See p. 90 of this edition.] See Father Hogan's interesting extracts in *Analecta Bollandiana,* ii. 49. I have translated the passage in *Ireland and the Celtic Church,* p. 86. The incident happened at Croghan, in Roscommon, the ancient seat of the Connaught kings. Every one knows, of course, that the institution of monks and nuns living in societies, sprang up in the latter part of the third century. A handy account of the origin of such monastic societies will be found in the article *Monasticism* in the new edition of the *Encyclopædia Britanica ;* or in the article *Monastery* in Smith and Cheetham's *Dictionary of Christian Antiquities.* (*G. T. Stokes.*)

25. From this passage onward to the bracket in § 23 in chap. v., is omitted in the Book of Armagh, but is supplied from the Cottonian and other MSS.

26. So the Cottonian MS. reading *una causa.* So the Bollandist reading, although Hamilton has omitted the words.

27. *A nutu Dei,* translated as above by Sir S. Ferguson

Nicholson, Olden, &c. Hennessy renders simply 'from God.' The Bollandist text has *a nuntio Dei.*

28. The Cottonian MS. is *ut esset virgo Christi, et ipsa Deo proximaret,* which we have translated. The Bollandists read *ut permaneret virgo Christi, et sic Deo proximaret.* Hamilton renders the latter 'who advised her to remain a virgin of Christ, and thus draw near to God.'

29. Lat. simply *illud.* Hamilton paraphrases, 'that grace.'

30. The meaning of the Latin expression *de genere nostro* is somewhat obscure ; probably the reference is to his converts as his spiritual children.

31. Compare 2 Tim. iv. 18, but that passage is not directly cited here.

32. Lat. *a fide.* Hamilton, incorrectly, 'from my purpose.'

33. Rom. viii. 7. Patrick uses *caro inimica ;* the Vulgate, *sapientia carnis inimica.*

34. The Cottonian MS. has *quare vitam perfectam ego non egi.* The Bollandist edition has *quod ego vitam perfectam non dedici,* curiously rendered by Hamilton 'that I have not studied eternal life.'

35. 2 Tim. iv. 8. The Latin is *fidem servavi.*

CHAPTER 'V.

1. The Latin is *novit omnia etiam ante tempora secularia.* The last phrase occurs in the Vulg. of 2 Tim. i. 9, whence Archdeacon Hamilton gives a reference to that passage. But the passage in Acts xv. 18 is on the whole nearer in meaning, although not quoted here with verbal accuracy.

2. Hamilton considers there is some gap here in the narrative, but the supposition is unnecessary.

3. Lat. *in milia milium.* Hamilton renders 'on account of many thousands.'

4. Literally 'on account of my rusticity.' The Latin is *propter rusticitatem meam.*

5. The Cottonian MS. has *nunc mihi capit.* The Bollandist has *nunc mihi sapit,* rendered by Hamilton 'it is delightful for me.'

6. The Latin is *utinam ut et vos imitemini majora, et potiera faciatis,* doubtfully rendered by Hamilton 'would to God that you would imitate me in holier things and do them more wisely.'

7. Prov. x. 1 ; xv. 20, but the Vulgate rendering is there, 'a

wise son maketh the father glad.' The Itala version of the passage is not extant.

8. Compare 1 Thess. ii. 10, but the passage is only referred to, not quoted.

9. The words are *ego fidem illis præstiti* (Cott. MS., *præstavi*) *et præstabo*. Hennessy renders : ' I have given the faith to them, and I will continue to do so.' And similarly Hamilton.

10. See Lev. xxiv. 16, but only the substance and not the words of that text is quoted. The words of the Apostle in Rom. ii. 24 were also evidently in Patrick's mind.

11. So the Book of Armagh reads *in nominibus*. Other MSS. *in omnibus*, ' in all things,' and so Hamilton and Olden. Sir S. Ferguson follows, however, the former reading, translating ' in words.'

12. Lat. *ultronea munuscula.*

12b. ' The screpall was an ancient Celtic coin, value about threepence, weighing twenty-four grains. See Petrie's *Round Towers*, p. 214.' (*Hennessy.*) There is evidently a reference to 1 Sam. xii. 3 ; 1 Kings xii. 3 (*Douay Version*).

13. When Patrick made his first journey into Connaught, he bargained for a safe conduct with Endeus, a chief, from the plain of Domnon, near the wood of Fochlut, near Killala, in Mayo. See Tirechán's account of this incident in the Book of Armagh, printed by Father Hogan in *Analecta Bollandiana*, ii. 42. Patrick on that occasion paid the price of fifteen slaves for the services of Endeus. (*G. T. Stokes.*)

14. The Latin *et nihil comprehenderunt me* can scarcely be explained with Hennessy to mean ' and who understood nothing but (to protect) me.' For, as Hennessy states in his note, Villanueva reads correctly *nihilominus* instead of *nihil. Nihil* must have been understood in the sense of *nihilominus* by Patrick. The Bollandists also read *nihilominus.*

15. These judges were Brehons. The Brehon law lasted in force till the reign of James I. The Brehon laws have been published by the Government under the guidance of eminent Celtic scholars like Dr. O'Donovan, Mr. O'Curry, Drs. Ritchie and O'Mahony. Dr. Atkinson, of Trinity College, Dublin, is now at work upon the completion of this great work. Sir Henry Maine, in his *Ancient Law*, chap. x., and in other works, gives an interesting account of the provisions of the curious code to which Patrick here refers. (*G. T. Stokes.*) The Cottonian MS. has *illis qui judicabant*, but the Bollandists read *eis qui indigebant*. Hence Hamilton has, ' how much I bestowed amongst those who were in distress.'

16. The Latin is *non minimum quam pretium quindecim hominum*

distribui illis. Hamilton quite incorrectly renders the clause 'I have distributed among these men not less in amount than in value.'

17. Here ends the portion that is added from the Cotton an MS. (See note 25, chap. iv.) The passage quoted is 2 Cor. xii. 15.

18. This clause is added from the Cottonian MS. It is not in the Armagh or Bollandist texts.

19. Some MSS. 'neither have I written to you that there may be an occasion of praise or gain from you.'

20. So the Book of Armagh, but other MSS. have ' which is not seen, but is believed with the heart, but faithful is He who promises [and] never lies.' Comp. Heb. x. 23.

21. There is an allusion here to 2 Cor. xii. 7, but no quotation. The phraseology is not as similar in the Latin as might be inferred from the English.

22. 1 Cor. iv. 3. The words of the Latin of that passage are here quoted, *neque meipsum judico.* The word *dignum* is supplied in square brackets [ ] in the Rolls *Tripartite,* p. 373, and is supplied, also in brackets, in Nicholson's text of the Bollandists. But it is quite unnecessary. Hamilton omits the words in his translation.

23. From here to end of the second paragraph in § 25 is omitted in the Book of Armagh.

24. The words are quoted from Acts xx. 24, as is seen from the Latin *sed nihil horum vereor.*

25. The Cottonian MS. reads 'because,' *i.e., quia* for *qui.*

26. Psa. lv. 22 (Psa. liv. 23, *Douay Version*), but the wording is a little different from the Vulgate and the Itala : *jacta cogitatum tuum in Dominum,* instead of *jacta super Dominum curam tuam.*

27. Gal. ii. 6, but that passage is only referred to. Comp. Prov. xviii. 5.

28. Psa. cxvi. 12 (Psa. cxv. 12, *Douay Version*).

29. Dr. Whitley Stokes gives *nihil valeo* as the reading of the Cottonian MS. This is the reading also of the Bollandists. Other MSS. *nihil video,* 'I see nothing.'

30. Other MSS. read : 'to lose his people whom I have gained.' Dr. Whitley Stokes notes that in the Armagh MS. *suam* is written over *meam.*

31. Lat. *lucratus sum animam cum corpore meo.* The context shows that St. Patrick refers to the resurrection, and therefore Hamilton's translation is incorrect, ' that by the loss of my body I should save my soul.'

32. Hosea i. 10. The Cottonian MS. has 'the Son of God.'

33. The last clause 'for of Him,' &c., is omitted in the Cottonian MS., but is found in two MSS.

34. Lat. *neque permanebit splendor ejus.* Hamilton renders
'and its splendour shall be dimmed.'

35. Lat. *in pænam miseri male devenient.* Therefore Hamilton's translation is too strong, 'shall perish unceasingly for all
eternity.'

36. Lat. *solem verum Jesum Christum.* Not, as Hamilton,
'Jesus Christ the true Sun of Justice.'

37. Lat. *interibit*, not, as Hamilton, 'never shall go down.'

38. Some MSS. omit 'as Christ continues for ever.'

39. Compare 1 Tim. v. 21, although that passage is not quoted,
but imitated here.

40. Here end the paragraphs inserted from the Bodleian MSS.,
but not found in the Book of Armagh.

41. The Armagh MS. omits 'the will of God.'

42. Hennessy has the following note on this paragraph :
'This sentence is separate from the text in the Book of Armagh,
but seems written by the same hand.—T.O'M. [Thaddeus
O'Mahony]. Ware does not give it, but quotes it in a note.'

THE EPISTLE TO COROTICUS.

1. The title of this Epistle in Dr. Whitley Stokes' work is
'The Epistle of St. Patrick to the Christian subjects of the
tyrant Coroticus.'

2. Coroticus was a Welsh prince. Some twenty years ago a
pillar was discovered in Wales, with the name Coroticus in Latin
and Ogham. Some have identified this with the name of
Patrick's correspondent. (*G. T. Stokes.*)

3. The reference is to 1 John iii. 15, but there is no direct
quotation. Patrick writes *in morte vivunt*, while the New
Testament phrase is *manet in morte.*

4. The Picts inhabited Scotland, and were also scattered over
the north of Ireland. Comgall of Bangor and Canice of
Kilkenny were Irish Picts. Columba was a Scot ; he summoned
Comgall, the founder of Bangor, and Canice, to help him in
preaching the Gospel to the Scottish Picts, recognising the fact
that community in blood and language is a great help towards
persuasion. There is a tradition that the Picts of Scotland
accepted Christianity before Patrick's day, but soon fell away

again into Paganism. Hence Patrick calls them apostate Picts.
See Bede, *Hist. Eccles.* iii. 4 ; Ussher, vi. 200, 210. (*G. T. Stokes.*)

5. The early Christians always wore white robes in church
after their baptism, and were anointed at their baptism and at
their confirmation. The Gallican and Irish Churches of
Patrick's time used only one unction, either at baptism or
confirmation. The Roman Church used unction on both occasions. This was one of the great points of difference between
Augustine and the Celtic Church of Britain, in the seventh
century. See Hefele's *History of Councils*, iii. 160 (Clark's
Translation). There is a reference to these baptismal customs
in the story about the conversion of King Leary's daughters at
the well of Croghan referred to in note 24, chap. iv. (*G. T.
Stokes.*) See the story on p. 90 ff.

6. John viii. 34. The correct text is, ' Whosoever committeth
sin is the servant (slave) of sin.' See also verse 44.

7. Almost after Psa. xiv. 4 (Psa. xiii. 4, *Douay Version.*)
Patrick's version agrees with neither the Vulgate nor Itala.

8. Psa. cxix. 126 (Psa. cxviii. 126, *Douay Version.*)

9. Dr. Whitley Stokes inserts as above *aliena, sed* within
brackets. The reference is to 2 Cor. x. 15.

10. Matt. xviii. 18, though the quotation is not exact. We
cannot agree here with Patrick's interpretation, and may repeat
what we have elsewhere written on the subject. The power
given to the Church (John xx. 23) seems to have been simply
to declare, by the preaching of the Gospel, forgiveness to all
who would believe in Christ. Our Lord's words were not
addressed on that occasion especially or entirely to the apostles,
since one apostle was not present, namely, Thomas (John xx.
24) ; and several who were not apostles, such as Cleophas and
his companion (Luke xxiv. 33–36),—and probably the holy
women also,—were in the assembly to which our Lord addressed
the words recorded in John xx. 23. The substance of the commission then given to the Church is given in general terms in
Luke xxiv. 47. (See also Mark xvi. 16.) According to the
usage of Scripture *prophets* are frequently said to *do* themselves
that which they were commanded to *announce* that God would
bring to pass. (See 1 Kings xix. 17 ; Jer. i. 10 ; Hosea vi. 5 ;
Rev. xi. 5, 6.) The power of binding and loosing, which
Patrick here refers to, given to Peter (Matt. xvi. 19), and to the
other apostles as representatives of the Church (Matt. xviii. 18),
was that of declaring by the power of the Holy Ghost what
ordinances of the law of Moses were binding on Christians, and
what had ceased to be so. It is well known that in the phraseo-

logy of the Jews, which was common in our Lord's day, to *bind* means *to declare prohibited*, and *to loose* is *to declare lawful* or *permitted*. See Lightfoot, *Horæ Hebraicæ*. Instances of the exercise of such power are given in Acts xv. 28, 29 ; Rom. xiv. 5, 6, 14, 17, 20 ; 1 Cor. viii. ; Gal. v. 1, 2 ; Col. ii. 16, 17.

11. The quotation is from Ecclus. xxxiv. 23, 24. It coincides with the Vulgate and Itala, save that the word *reprobat* in the first verse is used in place of *non probat*, which we have indicated by substituting 'reprobates' for the Douay 'approveth not.'

12. The quotation is from Job xx. 15, 16, but it is only a loose paraphrase with peculiar additions ; the Latin is most ungrammatical.

13. The quotation is from Hab. ii. 6, but is not exact, though Patrick approximates nearer to the Itala than to the Vulgate.

14. A summary of the commandment in Exod. xx. 17. Compare Rom. xiii. 9.

15. 1 John iii. 14. The words 'his brother,' though omitted in the Vulg. and Itala (followed, of course, by the Douay Version) are yet found in this passage in many Greek MSS.

16. That is ' by our humble exhortations.'

17. Note the imitation here of 2 Cor. i. 15–17.

18. Dr. Whitley Stokes gives the reading of the Cottonian MS., *Numquid amo piam misericordiam quod ago erga gentem*, which is translated above. Hennessy gives the reading of that MS. to be *Numquid a me piam misericordiam quod ago*, &c., which would be, ' Was it from myself that pious compassion which I exhibit towards,' &c.

19. Decurions formed what we might call the local town councils in every small town and village about the year A.D. 400. The notice of this office constitutes an interesting incidental proof of the authenticity of this Epistle. I have given in my *Ireland and the Celtic Church*, p. 37, a full explanation of the office and many references to foreign works on the subject, which need not here be repeated. The same title Decurio, used here by Patrick, occurs twice in Hübner's volume of *British Latin Inscriptions*, Nos. 54 and 189. If the *Epistle to Coroticus* had been forged even a century later, the forger would have known nothing of ' decurions,' as the barbarian invaders of the Roman Empire substituted their own local organisation in the villages and smaller towns for that of the Romans. See Stubbs' *Constitutional History of England*, vol. i. chap. v. (*G. T. Stokes.*)

On Patrick's noble birth, and the references to it, see *Confession*, chap. iv. note 9.

20. Quoted from Ecclus. xxxiv. 28, but in that place the sentences are reversed, and participles are employed.

21. Compare 2 Cor. xii. 14, which passage evidently was passing through Patrick's mind.

22. See Jer. xvi. 16, compare the *Confession*, § 17.

23. *Quamobrem injuriam justorum non te placeat etiam usque ad inferos non placebit.* Dr. Whitley Stokes refers the pronoun *te* to God, for he adds *Domine* within brackets. But the sense given in our translation seems to us more natural. Sir S. Ferguson notes: *Ad inferos*, equivalent to the Irish use of *go brath*, to the condemnatory judgment, 'for ever.' Nicholson supposes a reference here to Prov. xvii. 15. The Bollandist edition reads 'he who does not appease Thee (Lord) on account of the injury done to the just, even to the lower regions he will not appease Thee.'

24. 'The Franks who invaded and conquered Gaul, and from whom it derives its modern name of France, did not embrace Christianity until A.D. 496, and therefore this Epistle, which speaks of them as still Pagans, must have been written before that date.' (*Olden.*)

25. So the Cottonian MS. But Nicholson has 'to send holy presbyters, suitable men, to the Franks and foreign nations.'

26. 'The *solidus* was a gold coin originally worth twenty-five denarii, but in the time of Patrick it was reduced to one-half its value, and was probably worth from seven to eight shillings.' (*Olden.*)

27. In this passage again we find another undesigned coincidence proving the authenticity of this letter. The *Epistle to Coroticus* was written when Patrick was now an old man, and after he had laboured for many years. It must have been written in the second half of the fifth century, at which period the northern and eastern part of Gaul were desolated by the invasions of the barbarians. It was then counted a most meritorious work to send contributions to purchase back the Christian captives made by the Pagan invaders. (*G. T. Stokes.*)

28. This expression seems to have been a common one with Patrick. It occurs again in the Notes of Muirchu (Rolls edition, p. 288) : 'I cannot judge, but God will judge,' *Non possum judicare sed Deus judicabit.*

29. Rom. i. 32 is here referred to, though not accurately quoted. Hennessy's text omits the Biblical quotation, which is given in the Bollandist text. The previous clause is slightly different in the Bollandist edition.

30. 1 Cor. xii. 26. The quotation, though substantially the same in meaning, agrees with neither the Itala nor the Vulgate.

31. This, if not partly a quotation, as is possible, is modelled after Psa. lxv. 3 (Psa. lxiv. 3, *Douay Version*). Patrick's words

are *prævaluit iniquitas iniquorum supra nos;* those of the Itala
and Vulgate, *verba iniquorum prævaluerunt supra nos.*

32. Copied from Psa. lxix. 8 (lviii. 8, *Douay Version*).

33. Patrick evidently speaks here in the name of his converts.
(See the *Confession,* chap. i. 1, and note 6, p. 125.)

34. The passage in Mal. ii. 10 was evidently here in the saint's
mind. He connected the thought there with the saying of the
Apostle in Eph. iv. 5, 6. It is noteworthy that he refers later in
this paragraph also to Mal. iv. 3, 4.

35. 'In vain,' *in vacuum,* agreeable to the Irish idiom *dul ar
nemnid.* (*Sir S. Ferguson.*) Compare Gal. ii. 2 ; iv. 11.

36. The quotation is composed of phrases from Rev. xxi.
4, 25.

37. Taken from Mal. iv. 3, 4 ; but the quotation, though
substantially the same, does not entirely agree with the Vulgate.
It is much nearer to the Itala version, which is : *et salietis sicut
vituli de vinculis relaxati, et conculcabitis iniquos, et erunt cinis
subter pedes vestros.* Patrick's version is : *exultabitis sicut vituli
ex vinculis resoluti, et conculcabitis iniquos, et erunt cinis sub pedibus
vestris.*

38. Rev. xxii. 15, but the quotation is not exact.

39. Rev. xxi. 8, slightly altered.

40. The passage quoted is 1 Peter iv. 18, but the quotation is
a free one.

41. So the Cotton. MS. Nicholson and Sir S. Ferguson, with
other MSS., read the whole clause : 'who distribute baptized
women and the spoils of orphans among their most depraved
satellites.' Dr. Whitley Stokes inserts this in his text within
brackets.

42. Nicholson has rendered the clause, *quod ego Latinum
exposui,* as in our version ; but in p. 168 of his work he has
explained it to mean 'which I have translated into Latin,' and
he draws the conclusion from thence that Patrick did not use a
Latin translation of the Bible, but translated the passage from
the Greek. The conclusion is, however, questionable (see remarks on p. 77), for the Latin may well be interpreted to mean
'which I have explained,' *i.e.,* I have explained in this Epistle
the purport of the Scriptures quoted.

43. Psa. lx. 6 (lix. 8, *Douay Version*).

THE CONFESSION OF TOURS.

1. The original is here 'rex regum, dominus dominantium,' which is an exact quotation (*et* only being omitted) of the Vulgate rendering of Rev. xix. 16.

2. The phrase here employed, 'arbiter omnis seculi,' conveys a deep thought, if we could regard the writer as fully conscious of the difference in meaning between the Latin words '*arbiter*' and '*judex*,' the former of which signifies one who gives judgment according to what is right and equitable, the latter, one who judges according to strict law.

3. The expression, 'magister gentibus,' here employed is somewhat peculiar.

4. 'Vita perpetua.'

5. 'Lætitia in veritate.'

6. 'Tu es exultatio in æterna patria.'

7. The original is here '*lux lucis*,' which must be distinguished from the Latin '*lumen de lumine*,' used as the translation of the expression in the Nicene Creed, φῶς ἐκ φωτός, which conveys the idea of Christ as the Light proceeding from the Father, the fountain of light.

8. 1 Tim. ii. 4, the portion enclosed within inverted commas is identical with the Vulgate translation. Hence we have given the wording of the Rheims translation in the so-called Douay Bible.

9. This is the Douay rendering of Ezek. xviii. 21, as the Latin of the original of the words under quotation marks is identical with the Vulgate of that passage, 'vita vivet et non morietur.'

10. Lat. 'in omni corde.'

11. Lat. 'multiplicata sunt delicta mea super me.' Such passages as Isa. lix. 12 and Psa. xl. 12 may have been in the writer's mind, but there is no actual quotation of Scripture.

12. Lat. 'per nos.'

13. The Latin here is 'et quod velle nos dicimus, nostris actibus adprobamus.' M. Berger suggests that *nos* is a mistake for *non*. We have followed his suggestion in the translation above, but with some hesitation.

14. The Latin is 'quia in sacramentis tuis meus sensus infirmus est.' The words are easy to translate, though the meaning conveyed thereby is not quite clear.

15. Lat. 'qui ex nobis duro corde verba non suscipis.'

16. The Latin is here at fault. 'Jhesus Christus Dominus noster' is in the nominative, and not in the vocative case.

17. The Latin here is faulty, 'ego peccavi in cælo et in terra

et coram te.' The Vulgate in Luke xv. 21 has correctly
' peccavi in cœlum et coram te.'

18. Lat. ' luxoriam ' instead of ' luxuriam.'

19. Lat. ' peccavi per fornicationem et per gulam.'

20. Lat. ' peccavi per instabilitatem mentis fidei et per dubietatis
impietatem.'

21. Lat. ' peccavi per vagationem et per discretionem mentis
meæ.' In late Latin ' discretio' is sometimes used in the
meaning of *judgment*, perhaps here with the idea of straining
after matters too high. Comp. Psa. cxxxi.

22. The MS. has ' per observationem.' M. Berger corrects
' per [in]observationem.'

23. The Latin is, ' per amissionem bonorum constitutorum.'

24. The Latin is, ' per accidiam vanam et per stuporem mentis.'
' Accidia,' more correctly spelled ' acedia ' (see Du Cange's
Glossarium med. et infimæ Latin.), is the Greek ἀκηδία, *loss of
care*, and then *grief*, or *melancholy*, sometimes arising from ennui.
Jerome explains ' acedia ' as a disease common among monks.

25. Compare the references to *spells* and other divinations of
that kind in the Hymn of St. Patrick.

26. Lat. ' per scrutationem Majestatis Dei.'

27. Lat. ' per dominici diei operationes et per inlecebr[os]as
cogitationes.' So M. Berger corrects the MS. reading.

28. Lat. ' per tristitiam seculi,' a thought evidently borrowed
from 2 Cor. vii. 10, where the same expression is used in the
Vulgate.

29. Lat. ' et per amorem pecuniæ ; ' comp. 1 Tim. vi. 10, but
the Vulgate has there ' cupiditas ' and not ' amor pecuniæ.'

30. Lat. ' per commessationem.'

31. Compare the story of St. Patrick having refused the honey
offered in sacrifice to false gods, as told in his *Confession*, at p. 44.

32. Lat. ' sed habeo te sacerdotem summum ad quem confiteor
omnia peccata mea.'

33. Lat. ' Id tibi soli, Deus meus.'

34. Quoted exactly from the Vulgate version, Isa. l. 6 (in
English version, Psa. li. 4).

35. Lat. ' fletum.'

36. The Lat. is identical with that in Psa. l. 13 in the Vulgate
version ; the Psalm in the English version is Psa. li. 11.

37. Compare St. Patrick's references to the devil in the Epistle
to Coroticus, pp. 68 and 69.

38. Lat. ' doctrinam meam.'

39. A quotation from the Vulgate version, Psa. cxlii. 10, with
the insertion of the words ' tu es doctor meus et,' ' Thou art my
teacher and.' The Psalm in the English Bible is Psa. cxliii. 10.

St. Patrick's Hymn in Ancient Irish.

FROM THE MS. LIBER HYMNORUM IN THE LIBRARY
OF TRINITY COLLEGE, DUBLIN.

*[The principal variants of the Bodleian MS. followed by
Dr. Whitley Stokes in the Tripartite Life are given in
the brackets.]*

Attomriug indiu niurt trén, togairm
    Trínóit
Cretim treodataid foirin [fóiritin *Bodl.
    MS.*] óendatad in Dúlemain Dail
Attomriug indiu niurt gene Crist cona-
    bathiur
    niurt [a *Bodl. MS.*] crochta conaad-
    nocul
    niurt n-ereirge co fhergabail
    niurt toniud do brethemnar bratha

Attomriug indiu niurt grad hiruphin
    in urlattaid aingel

Translation of St. Patrick's Hymn into the Modern Irish.

BY THE LATE

REV. JAMES GOODMAN, M.A.,

Professor of Irish in the University of Dublin.

Nasgaim me féin, a n-diu, le neart tréan, guiḋe na Tríonóide.
Creidim a d-trí pearsanna le h-adṁáil aondaċta Chruiṫuiġṫeóra an ḃreiṫeaṁnuis.
Nasgaim me féin a n-diu le neart gine Chríosd agus le na ḃaisde,
le neart a ċroċda agus a aḋluicṫe,
le neart a eiséirġe agus a ḋeasġaḃála
le neart a ṫeaċda ċum breiṫeaṁnuis lae an ḃráṫa.
Nasgaim me féin a n-diu le neart gráḋa Sheraḃín,

[ı ꝼꝛeꞃꞇaɩ nanaꞃchaɩᵹıuɩ *Bodl. MS.*]

hı ꝼꞃeꞃcıꞃın eꞃeıꝛᵹe aꞃ cenn ꞃoch-
ꞃaɩce

ın eꞃnaɩᵹꞇhıb huaꞃaɩ aꞇhꞃach

ı ꞇaıꞃceꞇɩaɩb ꝼaꞇha

hı ꞃꞃaɩceꞃꞇaɩb aꞃꞃꞇaɩ

ın hıꞃeꞃaɩb ꝼuıꞃmeꝺach

ın enꝺᵹa noem ınᵹen

hı nᵹnımaɩb ꝼeꞃ ꝼıꞃean

Œꞇomꞃıuᵹ ınꝺıu nıuꞃꞇ nıme

ꞃoıɩꞃe ᵹꞃ[eı]ne

eꞇꞃochꞇa ꞃnechꞇaı [éꞃcı *Bodleian MS.*]

ane ꞇheneꝺ

ꝺéne ɩócheꞇ

ɩuaꞇhe ᵹaeꞇhe

ꝼuꝺomna maꞃa

ꞇaıꞃıꞃem ꞇaɩmaın

cobꞃaıꝺechꞇ aıɩech

Œꞇomꞃıuᵹ ınꝺıu nıuꞃꞇ ꝺé ꝺom ɩuamaꞃ-
achꞇ

a n-uṁluiġeaċṫ aingeal,
a ḃ-ḟpearḋal na n-árḋaingeal,

a n-ḋóṫċar na h-eiréipġe mar luaċ-
raoṫaiṗ,
a n-uṗnuiġṫiḃ na n-áṫċaċ n-uaṡal,
a ḋ-ṫaiṗṗġipeaċṫ na ḃ-ṗáiṫeaḃ,
a ṗeanmónṫaiḃ na n-Eaṗbal,
a ġ-cpeiḋeaṁ na ḃ-ṗuiṗṁiḋeaċ,
a n-ġlaine na m-bannaoṁ,
a n-ġníoṁaiḃ na ḃ-ṗíṗéan.

Naṗġaim me ṗéin a n-ḋiu le neaṗṫ
    Neiṁe,
roluṗ ġṗéine,
ġille na ġealluiġe,
aoiḃneaṗ ṫeineaḋ,
ḋéine ṫinnṫeaċ,
luaiṫe ġaoiṫe,
ḋoiṁneaċṫ maṗa,
ṗeaṗṁaċṫ ṫalṁan,
ḋainiġne na ġ-caiṗġeaṫ.

Naṗġaim me ṗéin a n-ḋiu le neaṗṫ Ḋé
    ḋo'm ṗṫiúṗuġaḃ,

cumachta vé vom chumgabail
ciall vé voinm imchuɾ
poɾc vé vom peimciɾe [imcaiɾin

Bodl. MS.]

cluaɾ vé vom eɾtecht
bɾiathaɾ vé vom eɾlabɾai
lam vé voimm imvegail
intech vé vom pemthechtaɾ
ɾciath vé vom vitin
ɾochpaite vé vomm anucul
aɾ intlevaib vemna
aɾ aɾla:gthib vualchet
aɾ iɾnechtaib [Bodl. MS. foiɾmvech-
aib] aicniv
aɾ cech nvuine mivúɾ thɾaɾtaɾ vam
i cein ocuɾ inocuɾ inuathev ocuɾ hi
ɾochaive

Tocuiɾiuɾ etɾum thɾa na [Bodl. MS.
inviu inna] huile neɾtɾo [Bodl.
MS. neuɾtaɾa]
fɾi cech neɾt namnaɾ netɾocaɾ

cúṁaċṫ Ṫé ṫo'm ċonġḃáil ṛuaṛ,
ciall Ṫé ṫo'm ṫṛeóṛuġaḋ,
ṛúil Ṫé ṫo'm ḟaiṛe,

cluaṛ Ṫé ṫo'm éiṛṫeaċṫ,
bṛiáṫaṛ Ṫé le laḃaiṛṫ aṛ mo ṡon,
láṁ Ṫé ṫo'm ċoṛnaṁ,
ṛlíġe Ṫé ṛoṁam,
ṛciaṫ Ṫé ṫo'm ṫíṫean,
ṛluaġ Ṫé ṫo'm anacul
aṛ ṫoluiṫ ṫeaṁon,
aṛ ṁeallṫóiṛeaċṫ ṫuḃáilceaḋ,
aṛ ḟoṛmaṫaiṫ aiṛne,

aṛ ṛaċ n-ṫuine iaṛṛaṛ mo ṫíoġḃáil,
a ṛ-cein nó a n-ṛaṛ ṫom,

a n-aonaṛ nó le ṛluaġ.

Cuiṛim a n-ṫiu na neaṛṫa ṛo uile
    iṫiṛ me-ṛéin aṛuṛ ṛaċ neaṛṫ naiṁṫe-
    aṁuil eaṫ-ṫṛócaiṛeaċ ṫiocṛaḋ a n-
    aġaiṫ mo ċuiṛṛ nó m'anama:

fristi dom churp ocus domm an-
main
fri tinchetla [*Bodl. MS.* tairchetlaib]
saibḟathe
fri dubreċtu gentliuchta
fri saibrechtu heretecda
fri himcellacht nidlaċta
fri brichta ban ocus goband ocus
druad
fri cech fiss ara chuiliu [*Bodl. MS.*
adds corp ocus] anman duini
Crist domm imdegail indíu ar neim
ar loscud 7 ar badud ar guin
comchair [*Bodl. MS.* coimraib] ilar
focraice
Crist lim, Crist rium [*Bodl. MS.* re-
mam], Crist im degaid,
Crist innium, Crist issum, Crist uasum

Crist dessum, Crist tuathum,

Crist illius, Crist isius [*Bodl. MS.*
ipsius], Crist inerus,

a n-aᵹaiᵭ ċairpᵹipeaċ ᵰaiᵭeaᵭ ᵱall-
ᵱa,

a n-aᵹaiᵭ ᴅuᵬpeaċᴅa páᵹánaċ,

a n-aᵹaiᵭ ᵱaoᵬ-peaċᴅa eipiceaċ,

a n-aᵹaiᵭ cimceallaċᴅ ioᵭalaᵭpuiᵭ,

a n-aᵹaiᵭ piᵱeóᵹa ban, aᵹuᵱ ᵹaiᵬneaᵭ
aᵹuᵱ ᴅpuaᵭ,

a n-aᵹaiᵭ ᵹaċ ᵱeaᵱa ᴅo ċpuaillᵱeaᵭ
coᵱp aᵹuᵱ anam an ᴅuine.

Cpíoᵱᴅ ᴅo'm ċoᵱnaᵬ a n-ᴅiu aᵱ ᵹaċ ᵹné
neiᵬe,

aᵱ loᵱᵹaᵭ, aᵱ ᵬáċaᵭ, aᵱ ᵹuin,

nó ᵹo ᵬ-ᵱaᵹainn iomaᴅ luaiᵭeaċᴅaᵭ.

Cpíoᵱᴅ liom, Cpíoᵱᴅ póᵬam, Cpíoᵱᴅ am
ᵭiaiᵹ,

Cpíoᵱᴅ ionnam, Cpíoᵱᴅ ᵱúm, Cpíoᵱᴅ
oᵱ mo ċionn,

Cpíoᵱᴅ aᵱ mo ᵭeiᵱ, Cpíoᵱᴅ aᵱ mo
láiᵬ ċlé,

Cpíoᵱᴅ a leiᵭeaᴅ, Cpíoᵱᴅ a ᵬ-ᵱaiᴅe,
Cpíoᵱᴅ a n-aoiᵱᴅe,

Cpípt i cpíoiu cech ouine imim
impopoa [*Bodl. MS.* pooom-
rcpiutaoap],

Cpípt ingin cech oen [*Bodl. MS.*
ouine] po oom labpathap,

Cpípt in cech pupc [*Bodl. MS.*
ipupcc cech] nom oepcaeoap
[*Bodl. MS.* ouine pooomoeca-
oap]

Cpípt in cech cluaip pooam chlo-
athap

Attompiug inoiu niupt tpén, togaipm
Tpinoit

Cpetim tpeooataio poipitin oenoatao
in Oulemain oail [The Dubl. MS.
has here only the initials p. o. i. o.]

Oomini ept palup, Oomini ept palup,
Chpipti ept palup,

Salup tua Oomine pempep nobipcum.

Cpíoꞃo a ᵹ-cꞃoiꞇe ᵹaċ n-ouine ꞃmuai-
neaꞃ opm,

Cpíoꞃo a m-béal ᵹaċ n-ouine laḃꞃaꞃ
liom,
Cpíoꞃo a ꞃúil ᵹaċ n-ouine ꝼéaċaꞃ
opm,

Cpíoꞃo a ᵹ-cluaiꞃ ᵹaċ n-aon ċloiꞃꝼeaꞃ
me.
Naꞃᵹaim me ꝼéin a n-oiu le neaꞃꞇ ꞇꞃéan,
ᵹuiꞇe na Tꞃíonóioe.
Cꞃeioim a o-ꞇꞃí peaꞃꞃanna, le h-aoṁáil
aonoaċoa Cꞃuiꞇuiᵹꞇeóꞃa an ḃꞃeiꞇe-
aṁnuiꞃ.

Oomini eꞃꞇ ꞃáluꞃ, Oomini eꞃꞇ
ꞃáluꞃ, Cꞃiꞃꞇi eꞃꞇ ꞃaluꞃ.
Saluꞃ ꞇua Oómine ꞃiꞇ ꞃempeꞃ
nobiꞃcum. Amen.

[N.B.—The Rev. Professor Abbott, of Trinity College, Dublin, has kindly collated the Dublin MS. for me.]